Chichester city walls

Andrew Westman

Chichester
city walls

Andrew Westman

Published by Museum of London Archaeology 2012
Copyright © The Chichester City Walls Project

www.chichestercitywalls.org

© Chichester District Council

A CIP catalogue record for this book is available from the British Library

Design and production by Tracy Wellman
Reprographics by Andy Chopping
Editing by Sue Hirst/Susan M Wright
Copy editing by Wendy Sherlock
Printed by Butler Tanner and Dennis Ltd

Front cover: Chichester walls and cathedral

Contents

Acknowledgements

The City Walls Partnership commissioned Museum of London Archaeology (MOLA) to write and produce this book as part of a programme of conservation and celebration of the city's walls funded, in part, by the Heritage Lottery Fund. It would not have been possible to research and write the story of the walls without the encouragement and support of the City Walls Project Officer, Andy Howard, and the information and advice provided by the District Council's Historic Environment Record Officer, Ian Scrivener-Lindley and Archaeology Officer, James Kenny. The latter has been most generous with ideas, and to him is owed, in particular, the projection of the surveyor's lines preceding the establishment of the Roman town (Chapter 2). They have also obtained archaeological photographs, some of them published for the first time. George Anelay, Chichester's Community Archaeologist until 2011, also very generously discussed the results of the excavations he led to the west of the Palace bastion in 2010. Rob Symmonds, director of Fishbourne Roman Palace and Museum, and Tracey Clark, at Chichester District Museum (now 'The Novium'), assisted the project by providing photographs and other information. Considerable research in West Sussex Record Office was carried out by colleagues in MOLA, Rupert Featherby and Helen Dawson, to whom grateful thanks are due, and they would like to express their own thanks to the staff of the Record Office for the help they received there. In MOLA the project management was by David Bowsher and book design and production by Tracy Wellman, maps and plans were drawn by Carlos Lemos, some of the photographs of Chichester were taken by Andy Chopping, editing was by Sue Hirst and copy editing by Wendy Sherlock.

The City Walls Partnership includes Chichester District Council, Chichester City Council, Chichester Walls Walk Trust, The Chichester Society, Chichester Residents Association Coordinating Group, The Dean and Chapter Chichester Cathedral and The Church Commissioners for England.

1

Introduction

The purpose of this book is to narrate and explain the history of the city walls of Chichester, and especially to describe the evidence for their history. Much of the walls survives in one form or another, and the visible circuit is a conspicuous landmark, well known to people who live and work in Chichester and to the city's many visitors.

Until relatively recently, historically speaking (the early 19th century), most of the city was within the circuit of the walls, and today this circuit still defines the modern city centre. The walls are therefore, a physical sign of Chichester's long history as a city, from at least Roman times onwards. The historic significance of the walls has led to them being scheduled as an ancient monument and, more recently, to the preparation of a plan for their better conservation and their enjoyment by the public. The history of the walls, in the form of the present book, is one part of this plan.

It is important to know that for most of their history Chichester's walls have been much more than simply walls of masonry, as they appear now. The circuit has usually comprised at different times an earth bank inside the masonry walls, one or more broad ditches around the outside of the walls, gates where the four principal roads of the city cross the walls, a walk along the top of the walls protected by a crenellated parapet and at times, bastions or towers attached to the outer face of the walls. In this account, unless otherwise specified, the term 'walls' (in the plural) means some or all of these elements.

The walls have for a long time defined and served to protect Chichester, and therefore their history is naturally bound up to a large extent with the history of the city. The walls cannot be understood in isolation, and need to be seen in the context of the city and its surroundings. Nevertheless this account is not a history of Chichester, as such, but rather of the city's walls in their historical, cultural, economic and military context.

After the present introduction this account consists of nine chapters arranged in chronological order, starting with Chapter 2 to set the scene in the 1st century AD, when Chichester was founded soon after the Roman invasion of Britain. The Roman town may have existed for as long as 200 years before walls were built around it, although exactly when and why the town should have been made defensible in this way remain important, open questions. In any case, defending the Roman town was clearly a substantial and expensive undertaking. Chapters 3 and 4 describe how the walls were first built and how subsequently these defences were augmented with bastions or towers.

Britain's connection with the Roman world lapsed in the 5th century AD, and in time the previously mainly Celtic-speaking Romano-British population was partly displaced, and partly absorbed, by English-speaking immigrants into eastern and southern Britain.

Eventually Sussex, the kingdom of the South Saxons, came into existence, one of several regional English kingdoms. Being relatively small and situated on the coast, Sussex was exposed to the seaborne depredations of Vikings and Danes. Chichester seems to have been practically empty of people until nearly the end of the 9th century AD. The existence of the walls of the former Roman town was probably why Chichester was chosen to be made into a 'burh', one of 30 or more defensible bases in southern England from which the Danes could be resisted, described in Chapter 5.

By the late 10th century AD the various regional English kingdoms, like Sussex, had been merged into a single English kingdom, although for another hundred years this was subject to attempted political or military takeover by overseas neighbours, Danes, Norwegians and Norman-French. Chapter 6 describes how, after the Norman Conquest of 1066, the western half of Sussex was put largely under the control of a single Norman-French lord, who in turn owed feudal loyalty to the king. The lord, Roger of Montgomery, and others like him, constructed numerous small castles across the country, and he had such a castle built in Chichester, inside the north-eastern corner of the walls, the better to collect taxes and enforce Norman rule. The status of Chichester was also confirmed by the foundation, on royal orders, of a cathedral in the south-west quarter of the city; it became the seat of a diocese that covered the whole county, replacing previous Anglo-Saxon minster churches in the region.

A flurry of activity occurred around the year 1200, when civil war in England and consequent intervention by the king of France threatened the safety of Chichester, which by then was a thriving market town and the most important place in the western half of Sussex. The castle was dismantled in c 1217, lest it fall again into the hands of the English king's enemies. The walls, which more obviously protected the townspeople, were a different matter. Chapter 7 recounts how the walls were subsequently rebuilt during the medieval period, especially in the face of attacks on southern England by France and its allies during the Hundred Years War. Even so, it seems that the only occasion on which the city's defences were subsequently put to the test was in the English Civil War, in the middle of the 17th century, when a Parliamentary army besieged the city, then being held by a Royalist garrison. Chapter 8 describes how, after several days' bombardment, the Parliamentary forces, threatening to break through the defences, received the surrender of the Royalists and took control of the city. In 1659, amid the uncertainty at the end of a period of government by parliament and army, without a king, Chichester's walls came close to being demolished, but in the event they were left intact. The next year a constitutional monarchy was restored and parliament's political supremacy was confirmed. Subsequently, the outbreak of war with the Dutch, whose strength lay in their navy, and then the possibility of war with other countries, especially France, would have argued against hasty removal of civic defences that could yet prove vital to a city so close to the sea.

Life for the people of Chichester was changing in other ways, too. The walls of Chichester no longer had as much immediate military and defensive value as before, but a new factor came into play, which was their value as a public amenity and civic ornament. By the early 18th century, the ditches were filled in and the upstanding wall, at least on the north-west and north-east sides of the city, was remade and planted with trees to form a series of prominent and shaded public walks, described in Chapter 9. The 18th century saw considerable prosperity in Chichester, the proof of which was the extent of the rebuilding, or at least the refacing, of its houses. It was fortunate for the survival of the city's walls that brick was the preferred building material for this work, rather than stone, or else the walls might have been robbed of what little stone was left in them.

The four principal gates, which constricted the flow of traffic into and out of the city, were demolished towards the end of the 18th century. Subsequently, there was no pressing reason to alter the walls and thereby diminish the city's amenities. The last chapter accounts for the survival of the walls through the 19th and 20th centuries. Only on the south-east were the walls demolished to any great extent, the line of the walls surviving in places merely as a property boundary. Expansion and improvement in the 19th century took place outside the circuit of the walls. Turnpike roads already had been made up to the gates, a canal from the harbour to the south of the city was opened in 1824 and in 1846 a railway line was built there connecting Chichester easily with London and therefore, increasingly, with the rest of the country.

The city's relative stagnation inside the walls during the 19th century left the streets and buildings there much as they had been a hundred years before. By the 20th century the result could be turned into a positive asset. The attractive and apparently unchanging character of the city centre, visibly defined by the circuit of its walls, attracted increasing numbers of visitors and tourists. Motor traffic began to be a problem, however, and a by-pass was constructed south of the city in 1939. Greater and more widespread affluence, especially

from the 1950s onwards, was marked by a huge growth in the ownership and use of cars. The environmental danger, as well as the economic and personal value, of car use began to be felt and Chichester became a national case study in the protection of a historic city without unduly limiting traffic. The construction of ring roads and relief roads in the 1960s and 1990s rerouted traffic away from the city centre, but entailed demolishing buildings next to the site of the west gate and brought traffic close to the south and west sides of the walls.

This account of the walls begins and ends with archaeology. For the early part of the history few or no documents exist to give us even the simplest and most essential information about the walls. Our best source is the physical remains of the walls themselves, as exposed and interpreted by archaeological intervention and understood in the context of other, comparable information from elsewhere. Later, when some events do come to be documented, we are faced with the problem of deciding how accurate and representative these documents are, and we can wonder what may yet have gone unrecorded; archaeology can still be vital to our understanding. The survival of the walls from the early 18th century onwards seems to be owed, at least in part, to a growing appreciation of them as a public amenity. From about that time, too, people began to recognise the great age of the walls. Antiquarians at first supposed them to have been Anglo-Saxon in origin, and only later discovered them to be Roman. The means of obtaining evidence to test such suppositions and to suggest other possibilities, as necessary, came with the growth and refinement of archaeology as a near-scientific discipline, from roughly the last quarter of the 19th century onwards. The history of the walls from that time forward thus includes the development of the means of understanding and writing the rest of their history. Accordingly, this account presents in the last chapter of this history some of the most instructive archaeological interventions as episodes themselves in the history of the walls. Chapter 10 is followed by 'Further reading', which identifies the main sources for our knowledge of the history of the walls, used to write the present book.

Archaeology, with some important technical exceptions such as scientific dating, is by no means an exact science and several critical matters in the history of Chichester's walls are still open to debate. As will be seen from the final chapter, every ten years or so since the Second World War the accumulation of more factual data has allowed one or other archaeologist to sum up the existing state of knowledge of the walls, bringing in more information and sometimes changing what hitherto had been received opinion. The present account includes little completely new information of that kind, and is based almost wholly on material already published. The main aim is to present a coherent history of Chichester's walls. Where uncertainty exists, as it often does, the account nevertheless leads with a reasonably likely line of argument, but other possibilities are also considered. This kind of book, therefore, cannot be the last word on its subject. Our knowledge of the walls, as of other aspects of Chichester's history, depends on the outcome of intermittent archaeological investigations, accumulating basic factual information little by little. Our understanding of the walls and their significance advances in a similarly incremental way, within a developing broader context of knowledge and scholarship. This history is inevitably a work in progress, and matters still in doubt may yet be answered or clarified in time to come.

1 **Plan of the historic centre of Chichester today**

publicly accessible areas of the walls

2

Setting the scene

NATURAL TOPOGRAPHY AND GEOLOGICAL BACKGROUND

Chichester is situated on the low-lying coastal plain of West Sussex, very close to sea level. The average height of the city is some 13m above Ordnance Datum (OD). About 4km to the north of the city, the South Downs begin to rise, reaching a height of more than 200m OD at the Trundle and Bow Hill, 2km further to the north. The Downs form high, smoothly rolling hills, ranged roughly from west to east: a solid barrier broken only by the narrow valleys of rivers cutting through them southwards to the coastal plain and the sea. By contrast with the rampart-like barrier of the Downs, the coastline is very irregular, both indented with estuarine creeks and embayments, and projecting sharply to the south of Chichester to form a low, flat promontory, culminating in Selsey Bill.

The local geology is especially relevant, as it determines what kinds of building stone are available for use in town walls or in any other structure. The solid geology under the coastal plain, originating millions of years ago, consists of clay and chalk that outcrop to the north, forming the Downs and, further north, the Weald. The much more recent overlying surface geology of the coastal plain comprises a series of overlapping deposits, ranged parallel to the Downs, of coombe rock, brickearth, sand and gravel. These deposits are generally subglacial or periglacial in origin, consisting of material eroded during or soon after the last Ice Age (from 110,000 to 13,000 years ago). The material derives from further inland, from along the length of the Downs or from the plains exposed to the south at a time when sea level was lower and the ground was more or less permanently frozen, only the surface

thawed in summer. Coombe rock is a common periglacial material, consisting of frost-shattered fragments of chalk and flints cemented in a matrix of chalky mud, while brickearth (so called for its suitability for brick-making) is a fine, silty clay containing occasional small flint pebbles, deposited by wind or water. In a warming climate, and after vegetation took hold, very fertile soils developed on these deposits. Some localised periglacial features, such as the hummocky terrain produced by thermokarsts, may have existed in places and were subsequently levelled by human activity if not natural agency.

The shoreline has been, and continues to be, the most obviously changeable element in the physical landscape. Since the end of the last Ice Age and the melting of enormous amounts of ice, some 13,000 to 12,000 years ago, the sea has risen an estimated 130m to reach its present level and, perhaps 5000 years ago, Britain became separated from the Continent of Europe. The advance of the sea has not been a simple process, however, progressing at a uniform rate. The rivers flowing through the chalk hills, having down-cut their valleys to reach a much lower sea level, began to deposit material, infilling their valleys and spreading it out over the plains below. The loss of permanent ice has permitted slow, upward eustatic movement of the land tending to counteract the earlier, rapid rise of sea level. The very latest

---

1   View from the Trundle hill fort across the coastal plain to the south-west with the irregular coastline and Isle of Wight in the background

deposits of alluvial silt and sand in the coastal plain mark a shifting zone, the meeting of rivers and tidal sea. Processes of erosion, by stormy seas, tides and currents, in tandem with processes of accretion, by silting from rivers and the transport of eroded material along the shore, have made the shoreline continually liable to move.

By the 1st century AD, when the history of Chichester as a recognisable town begins, there is no doubt that the coast was further away from the city than it is now, but its probable position can only be reconstructed conjecturally. The Selsey promontory is likely to have extended markedly further southwards, incorporating as land some features that are now banks and reefs offshore. The Mixon, a limestone reef now exposed at low water 1.5km south-east of Selsey Bill, would very probably still have been connected to dry land, together with sandbanks and shallows to its west. The Owers, two groups of rocks 4km and 11km out to sea to the south-east, would have been similarly connected once but may no longer have been by this time. Attempts have been made to reconstruct the coastline by extrapolating from the known rate of erosion in various places around Selsey over the last 300 years, which has amounted to as much as several metres a year, but the progress of erosion is unlikely to have been as straightforward as

such extrapolation assumes. The landform would have varied, and the processes of erosion would not have been uniform. Severe winter storms, for instance, could have breached shingle banks and flooded large areas in a single event.

Conversely, some areas of land along the coast that are now dry would have been under water in the 1st century AD, either all the time or at least at high tide. The water in river estuaries would tend to have ponded behind shingle and sand spits and bars. Some estuaries, such as that of the River Arun to the east of Chichester, probably met the sea in an irregular bay resembling, but smaller than, the present embayment of Pagham harbour, to the south of Chichester, where the River Lavant formerly flowed. Along the south coast to the east the low-lying areas of the Pevensey Levels would have been continually flooded and open to the sea. Generally, sea level was slightly lower than it is today, and the head of the eastern arm of Chichester harbour, now only 4km from the town centre, was then probably nearer Copperas Point, some 10km away. Nevertheless, the modern coastline immediately to the west of Chichester, still irregularly indented with long, shallow creeks and bays, gives a good impression of the character of the shoreline thereabouts in the 1st century AD.

The River Lavant flowed from the Downs and, under the natural conditions prevailing in the 1st century AD, meandered southwards to the sea within an ever-widening flood plain, just to the east of the site of Roman Chichester; the course of the river was later diverted to the west (Chapter 5). The river, then probably even more than now, was liable to flood rather unpredictably. The underlying natural geological deposits of chalk, sand and gravel easily hold water, but not far beneath them are impermeable strata of clay. Consequently the upper strata can quickly become saturated, causing any excess of water to flood the surface. In any case, ground water is generally very close to the surface in the area of Chichester. The site was always likely to have too much water at times, rather than too little.

HISTORICAL BACKGROUND

Our knowledge of the historical circumstances in which Chichester began life as a town, with or without walls, comes from a very few written sources and from a certain amount of archaeological evidence. Literary texts provide a crucial narrative account of events, although they were written sometimes long after the events they describe, and are often short, limited in scope and confusing. Archaeological evidence may include contemporary writing, such as the texts of inscriptions and on coins, but these may be cryptic and fragmentary. Other archaeological evidence on its own is simply neither detailed enough nor precise enough, especially with regard to dating, to give anything like this historical detail but it does supply complementary information which, interestingly, may often be information that contemporaries would not have been so clearly aware of.

AN IRON AGE *OPPIDUM*

The area around the present site of Chichester would have been fertile, well watered and agriculturally productive early in the 1st century AD, and probably well populated. The proximity of the coast would have meant that at least some of the population were sailors and fishermen, and sea traffic was certainly carried on along the shore and across the English Channel. Gaul, on the opposite side of the English Channel, had been brought under Roman control in the middle of the 1st century BC as a result of Julius Caesar's military campaigns, which had included two exploratory expeditions to Britain.

Roman writers tell us that the inhabitants of the area of Britain that included Chichester were called the Atrebates one of at least half a dozen Celtic peoples in southern Britain in the Late Iron Age, each forming a distinct polity with its own territory and leadership asserted by, among other things, the minting of coins. The Romans used the Latin word *civitas* for such a people and their polity, extending the meaning of a term they also used in a more Mediterranean context for city state and citizenry. The boundaries of these various territories tended to be rather imprecise and fluctuating, mainly as a result of chronic internecine conflict between the various polities, whose common culture

2 Location of Chichester, with places mentioned in the text

3 A small fragment of carved Roman masonry, perhaps with an inscription, reused in part of the city walls

4 Late Iron Age and Roman pottery from the cemetery at Westhampnett

promoted the leadership of a warrior aristocracy and the virtues of warfare. The territory of the Atrebates, based on a centre at Silchester (Hampshire), extended to the north at least as far as the Thames valley, where they were in conflict with another people, the Catuvellauni, who were aggressively expanding their territory from its original base at St Albans (Hertfordshire). The latter were already in the process of taking over the base of a third people, the Trinovantes, based at Colchester (Essex).

The most obvious sign of occupation at this time in the coastal plain near Chichester is a series of linear earthworks, known as the Chichester entrenchments or dykes. These earthworks comprise long stretches of a single ditch and a bank running side by side either roughly from west to east or from north to south, forming a more or less rectilinear pattern over a total area of several square kilometres to the north and north-east of the site of Chichester. The network is now recognised as extending between Bosham, on the west, and the River Arun, on the east, and is not obviously centred on Chichester, as had previously been assumed. The earthworks were extensively surveyed in the 1970s, although additions have been confirmed and apparent gaps have been resolved more recently. Excavations in various spots to expose sections and obtain datable finds have determined that much of the network of ditches and banks probably dates from late in the 1st century BC and early in the 1st century AD, although some ditches may have been cut, extended or, possibly, recut as late as the 16th century, to enclose the bishop's deer park.

5

In extent and character the Chichester dykes are strikingly like other Late Iron Age systems of ditches and banks near Winchester (Hampshire), Silchester, Canterbury (Kent) and, on a smaller scale, in two or three other places within 80km of Chichester, as well as elsewhere; the most elaborate and extensive examples are probably those west of Colchester and west of St Albans. The Romans called these earthworks *oppida*, using a Latin word for 'town', *oppidum*, and they also applied this term to more obviously defensive structures, especially hill forts, of which the Trundle, 2km north-east of Chichester, is an excellent example. There were many more hill forts much further to the west and north, most of which had a much longer history than the Chichester dykes and the other, similar, late 'territorial' *oppida*. The Chichester dykes are typical of the latter, covering a sizeable area on much flatter terrain, and generally they seem to have been at the centre of a tribal polity or *civitas*. As well as accommodating a royal clan and its many supporters, at least in time of need, these territorial *oppida* also contained sites of religious significance, perhaps to do with ancestors, water sources or a war god. It is uncertain if the economic activity that such a concentration of functions attracted should merit the description of a town, or a proto-town, although these places were the nearest thing to a town in Late Iron Age Britain. The locally minted coins may have been used as a store of wealth and to display loyalty, for instance, rather than as a medium of exchange.

6

The Late Iron Age earthworks north of Chichester, although very extensive, were often discontinuous and sometimes doubled up, one ditch and bank parallel to another. Even if their ends were prolonged, and the gaps were filled by natural obstacles such as thorn hedges, the practical defensive utility of these long ditches and banks is hard to see. It would be easy to assume that the Chichester dykes, for instance, protected the area they enclosed from the north and the east, but how would this protection have been effected? The ditches and banks would have kept out chariots, which were characteristically aristocratic war equipment employed mainly to carry warriors into and out of battle, but only large numbers of men could have taken advantage of the banks to try and keep attackers at bay who came on foot, or were themselves on horseback. Perhaps the purpose of the dykes was mainly symbolic, conveying a message that a particular polity could expend a huge amount of human energy to make the dykes, and therefore must be commensurately capable in war, if not able to defend the dykes directly. In later times the dykes came partly to be used as land boundaries, and this may have been another of their original functions, perhaps demarcating an enclosed area that was especially important to the *civitas* whose centre it was. Contemporaries may have believed that the area was thus protected in a non-material way, under religious sanction, or was neutral ground, suitable for a meeting place.

There is no definite evidence of a settlement or any other kind of occupation on the site of Chichester at this time, early in the 1st century AD, although intensive agriculture and settlement in the centuries since then will have obliterated much evidence. The centre of the Late Iron Age *civitas* represented by the Chichester dykes was probably situated in one or more places to the west and south of the later town. Perhaps the functions of the *civitas* did not require a single, physical centre and its important institutions, which coinage indicates must have included a mint were dispersed in several places; the very extent of the network of dykes would suggest this. A Late Iron Age sacred site existed on Hayling Island (Hampshire), for instance, on the west of Chichester harbour. Its excavated plan, a circular building surrounded by a large square enclosure, possibly a colonnaded ambulatory, and the abundance of votive objects left there, suggest that this was a place that attracted many worshippers. Other Celtic temples or shrines existed at Ratham Mill and at Broadbridge (both in Sussex) on a stream running south to Bosham, about 5km west of Chichester. In the opposite direction, north-east of Chichester, Iron Age coin moulds have been found at Boxgrove and a burial ground at Westhampnett (both in Sussex), the latter continued in use into the succeeding Roman period. There may have been places of political or religious importance at locations around the Selsey promontory now lost to erosion. Fishbourne (Sussex), at the head of the eastern arm of Chichester harbour, was to acquire great importance later (after the Roman invasion in AD 43). A retrospective argument may be dangerous, but the possibility of this site having importance before the invasion is strengthened by the existence of a substantial ditch of Late Iron Age date, containing an item of Roman military equipment. This ditch was subsequently infilled, but a timber-framed building (Building 3) constructed shortly afterwards had a very long life, lasting through all later phases of the site. Its function is not obvious, and it could have

had a non-utilitarian purpose. This area was very accessible by water, although the shoreline has subsequently moved inland. A deep water port probably existed off Copperas Point, which may already have acquired the practical importance that it seems to have had later (below).

The presence of a few pieces of Roman military equipment is not necessarily to be interpreted as indicating the presence of actual Roman soldiers, although before the invasion there may have been occasional official visitors or liaison officers. These items probably have the same significance as the one or two Roman coins and pieces of samian fineware found in the area, dating from some time before the invasion; namely that at that time the *civitas* of the southern Atrebates had close links with Gaul and its leaders were favourably disposed towards Rome.

7

8

---

5 Iron Age hill fort, the Trundle

6 A gold stater of the Catuvellauni, c 35 BC

7 Crop marks reveal the foundations of the Romano-Celtic temple at Hayling Island

8 Coin moulds and crucibles from the Iron Age settlement at Boxgrove

A ROMAN INVASION PORT

Since Caesar's expeditions in the mid 1st century BC, people on both sides of the English Channel seem to have been acutely aware of those on the other side, yet uncertain of their capabilities and intentions. The Romans, certainly, expected one day to complete what Caesar, the founder of Rome's new ruling dynasty, had begun; an invasion was planned by both Augustus and his successor-but-one, Gaius (Caligula), before being implemented under the next emperor, Claudius, in AD 43. The ostensible reason for invasion, or pretext if the Romans needed one, was the restoration to his throne of Verica, king of the Atrebates who, having been in alliance with Rome, had been deposed, possibly by the leader of the resurgent Catuvellauni. Verica had thereupon gone to Rome as an aggrieved exile. These political circumstances suggest that the Romans in Gaul already had direct, official contact with the leaders of the Atrebates, perhaps through the *oppidum* represented by the Chichester dykes, as well as trading contacts either directly or indirectly through intermediaries. Conversely, overthrowing the leadership of the Catuvellauni, based in their *oppidum* near Colchester, and subjugating their people would have been a major objective of the Romans' invasion. In any case the engine of the new Roman principate, a military autocracy dressed in the clothing of Rome's traditional republic, was its army, and political success and economic prosperity required wars of conquest. The invasion was expected to pay for itself and yield a profit, too.

A contemporary geographer, Strabo, wrote that Britain was rich in grain, cattle and hides, and gold, silver and iron, which were exported together with hunting dogs and slaves. These goods, including the slaves, who were presumably prisoners taken in the wars endemic among the British *civitates*, were probably shipped through the hands of either the Catuvellauni or the Atrebates. Wine, fine pottery and other luxuries obtained in return from Gaul and, through Gaul, from the rest of the Roman world were highly prized in Britain, conferring aristocratic prestige no matter what the attitude to Rome. Caesar had already noted, in the 1st

century BC, that the south coast was a source of iron, presumably coming from the Weald. The most valuable of these goods were probably exchanged as diplomatic gifts between aristocrats, and being in control of their supply would have given the Catuvellauni and the Atrebates appreciable influence.

The account of the invasion known to have been written not long afterwards by the historian Tacitus has not survived, and we depend for details mainly on much later, brief descriptions, notably by Dio Cassius, writing in the 3rd century AD. The most important, and plausibly correct, points are that the invasion sailed from the same port on the coast of Gaul as Caesar had done, Portus Itius (Boulogne, Pas-de-Calais), presumably to make the shortest crossing of the channel. The large Roman force, estimated at 40,000 men, with horses and equipment, was divided into three, in order to land at separate places. The main landing place was probably at Rutupiae (Richborough), then on the flat, sheltered, western coast of the Wantsum Channel in east Kent, where in due course a large fort of Claudian date was built. The other two

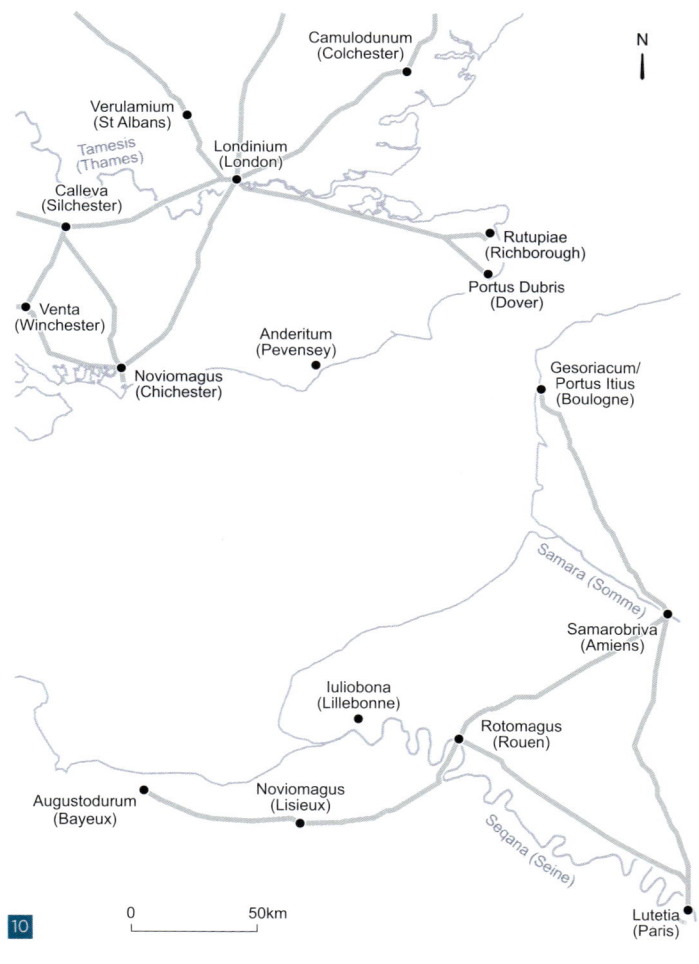

landing places are unknown, but it would have been politically logical for one to have been in the territory of the Atrebates, perhaps near Chichester, to take advantage of and to confirm the alliance with Rome. Wherever they landed, the divided forces should soon have recombined in order more effectively to overcome any opposition. The route taken by the Roman force has usually been identified as having gone through north Kent, crossing the River Medway and winning a battle there, and crossing the lower Thames somewhere just upstream of the site of London (ie the modern City of London and Southwark). After waiting there to be joined by the Emperor Claudius in person, the force went east to Camulodunum (Colchester), where the Romans decisively defeated their main initial enemy, the Catuvellauni. A different interpretation of the written sources, to the effect that the main invasion route went through the territory of the Atrebates and specifically by way of Chichester, although ingenious, is over-complicated, makes little geographical or strategic sense and can be convincingly refuted

After taking Camulodunum the Roman army turned to subdue other peoples who continued to resist them in the south-west of Britain, beyond the territory of the Atrebates.

The latter were able to give the Romans more help in this phase of the invasion. The Roman army constructed substantial timber-framed buildings, including granaries, at Fishbourne. The buildings date from the mid AD 40s, and functioned as a supply depot, one of several built to support the invasion and subsequent campaigns of conquest, and with the success of these campaigns the depots were dismantled. These depots were generally situated, as were the largest military camps, by a coastal anchorage or on a navigable river because as much material as possible would have been carried by water; this was much more practical and economical than transport overland, especially when permanent roads had not yet been made. The army would have built durable roads soon, however, and these would presumably have been laid out to serve the army's immediate purpose of waging war, as necessary, and the longer term purpose of controlling the indigenous peoples and requisitioning food and other materials from them. Without precise dating evidence, however, we must beware of making a circular argument, inferring the purpose by assuming an early date.

ROADS

The three earliest roads in the area of Chichester appear to be, firstly, a road running from south-west to north-east between Chichester and London (no. 15 in Ivan Margary's 1973 catalogue of *Roman roads in Britain*), known to us by its early medieval name of Stane Street; secondly, a road running westwards from Chichester in the general direction of Winchester (Margary 421); and, thirdly, another road running north from Chichester to Silchester (Margary 155). It used to be thought not only that all these roads had a common junction at Chichester but that this was their terminus, the implication being that Chichester was created at the same time as the roads, perhaps originating as a military base to protect an invasion bridgehead and the supply depot at Fishbourne, if not as a fully fledged town. Barry Cunliffe, writing in 1971, admitted this was a tempting interpretation while agreeing that not enough positive evidence of the early structures under the later town had yet been found to be sure, and this interpretation continued to be the general argument of, for instance, Alec Down's

---

9   Gold stater of Verica, found locally

10 The Channel coasts of Britain and Gaul, showing the position of Chichester (Noviomagus) and other towns

11 Bronze sestertius showing Claudius

12 Roman black colour-coated drinking goblet imported from Lezoux, central Gaul; found at the cattle market, Chichester

1988 book, *Roman Chichester*. More recently this interpretation, and the assumption that the Roman town of Chichester necessarily had a military origin in the same way as the main roads did, has been questioned.

An alternative argument proposes that the roads could have been laid out in the absence of a fort or similar military installations at Chichester, regardless of the possibility of a settlement there. Considered in this light, as if nothing yet existed at Chichester itself, the roads can be seen to have a different geographical logic. Evidence put forward by John Magilton in 1995 suggests that Stane Street was initially laid out running in a straight line across the site of the Roman town of Chichester and continued south-westwards to end probably on the east side of Chichester harbour, at or near Copperas Point. The latter may have been the nearest deep water anchorage at that time, reinforcing the implied purpose of this road as a supply road taking goods inland from the coast. Evidence for harbour installations at Copperas Point may have existed but has been lost to later erosion, just as the line of the road itself has been submerged by rising sea level, although a possible trace of it in the intertidal mud of Chichester harbour is detectable on aerial photographs. More evidence for this road line has been found on dry land to the east of Chichester harbour, while in the south-east quarter of the Roman town itself small areas of gravel road metalling have been excavated which, when first found, were interpreted as belonging to roads running from north to south, but equally can be interpreted as indicating a road running from south-west to north-east on the line of Stane Street. Indeed, these patches of road metalling could also represent road junctions. Stane Street itself runs across country to Southwark, on the south bank of the River Thames at London, which was then the lowest point on the Thames to which tides flowed and was therefore another deep water anchorage; it was also a point where the river could be safely crossed by ferry and, in due course, economically bridged. On the north bank of the Thames the road continued eastwards across country to Camulodunum (Colchester), which had been the principal objective of the invasion and was initially made the chief town of Roman Britain; we should think, therefore, of Stane Street as the southern leg of the main road to Camulodunum, initially, which happened to cross the Thames at Southwark and London. The course of the road immediately to the north-east of Chichester actually ran not in the direction of Southwark but further eastwards to Pulborough (Sussex), where a small settlement was therefore probably already in existence, and from there the road resumed a more direct route. When constructing a permanent road the Roman road surveyors could evidently deviate from the most direct line, which at the Southwark end of the road they were able to set out very accurately, in order to give access to appropriate places en route as well as to negotiate local terrain more conveniently.

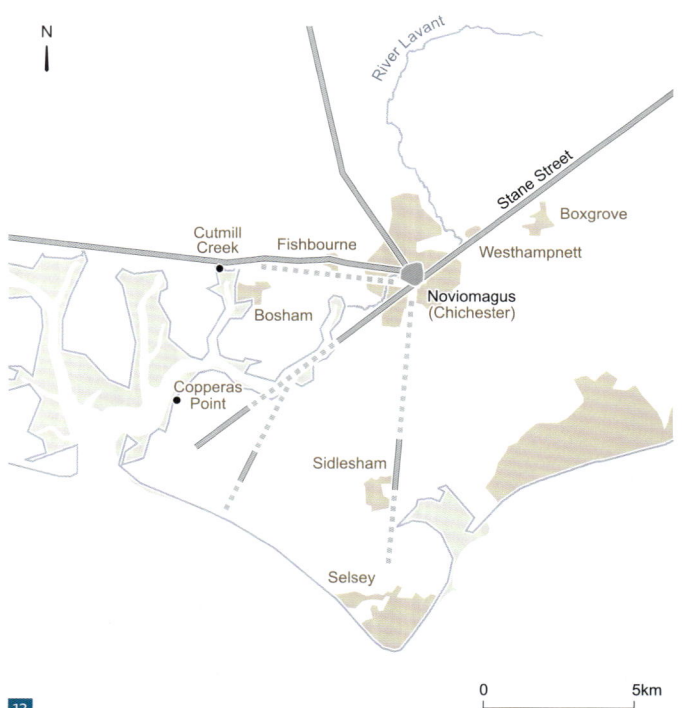

13

14

Stane Street may have been the first of these permanent roads to be built in the region of Chichester, if only because the other roads appear to have branched off it, although the likely existence of a Late Iron Age route between the *oppida* at Chichester and Silchester has been used to argue for the primacy of its Roman successor, the road north of Chichester. The course of this northern road is still uncertain immediately north of Chichester and excavations on what had been its presumed line, just to the west of Broyle Road (A286), have failed to find good evidence for it there. Roman cremation burials, to be expected near a road and not far outside a town, were found in 2008 to the east of Broyle Road, at Oaklands Park; equally significant were ditches running roughly from north to south, or more exactly, from slightly west of north to east of south, which may have been parallel to a road. This road is assumed to have been laid out in its final stretch so as to form the Roman precursor of North Street, within the town. If so, and if the ditches at Oaklands Park indicate its line there, the road would have had some minor changes of direction further to the south. This road would not have been laid out as it approached the site of Chichester by aiming for the north gate, as that did not exist then (as will be shown), but there may have been some landmark at that spot before the gate was built.

Another main road branching westwards from Stane Street appears to be more easily defined, as in time it became the main road from east to west inside the Roman town, a line still approximately followed by modern East Street and West Street. The greater length of this road has been well established to the west of Cutmill Creek, a point roughly 10km west of Chichester, where the Roman road has clearly determined the fairly straight line taken by the present road (A259), economically skirting the head of the various creeks and embayments along the coast. This long straight stretch of road and the east–west road in the Roman town are not in line, however. If the line of the straight stretch of the road west of Cutmill Creek is projected eastwards, towards Chichester, it runs directly through the site of the first Roman buildings at Fishbourne and, interestingly, along a contemporary metalled road excavated there. Further to the east this line runs to the south of, and almost parallel to, the east–west road in Roman Chichester and meets the line of Stane Street at a point on the south side of the

town. This point is also where the projected line of another Roman road would meet the line of Stane Street, namely the road (Margary no. 156) running roughly from north to south to Sidlesham (Sussex) and further on towards Selsey. Although the course of the latter road is uncertain in the immediate area of this putative junction, its line is well established further south. This road line is, moreover, exactly at a right angle to the road line projected from the west, and the line of Stane Street, running from south-west to north-east, practically bisects this right angle. These alignments are highly suggestive not of roads, in the first place, but rather of surveyor's lines taken across country, initially to apportion land and subsequently to lay out the roads required to demarcate and gain access to the various pieces of land. The relation between Stane Street and the other two intersecting road lines suggests that Stane Street probably came first, and both the other lines were then set out simultaneously from the line of Stane Street, at 45° to Stane Street and at right angles to each other. The area eventually occupied by the Roman town apparently lay wholly to the north of this intersection.

For a distance of some 6km east of Cutmill Creek, the line of the road west of Chichester is uncertain. The road may have run through Fishbourne at first but, if so, the road was later shifted northwards so that it would run through the middle of the Roman town. A deviation to the north took the road away from Chichester harbour and the immediate surroundings of Fishbourne, so, when the military supply depot was functioning during and soon after the invasion, the main road either ran directly through the depot or, if already shifted to the north, was met by side roads. When the town existed the east end of the main road was at its junction with Stane Street, under the eventual site of the east gate of the town. This junction and the east–west road there could conceivably have existed independently of, and prior to, the town and could have been set out before or after the depot at Fishbourne was dismantled.

FISHBOURNE PALACE
Wherever the focus of the Late Iron Age *oppidum* of the Atrebates had been, new and elaborate accommodation began to be built at Fishbourne, very near the site of the invasion-period military granary and supply depot, and not long after these short-lived buildings had been dismantled. This accommodation was built in stages, consisting of, firstly, a largely timber-framed set of buildings near the head of Fishbourne Channel, followed by, secondly, a stone-built villa comprising at least three large wings

ranged around a central garden, lavishly decorated in a style and with materials that would not have been out of place in Rome itself at that time. The likely purpose of this most unusual series of buildings, whose existence was unsuspected before their discovery in 1961, is to be understood in the historical context of the establishment by the Romans of a client kingdom encompassing a substantial area of southern Britain, centred on the territory of the Atrebates.

Some 30 years after these events Tacitus, writing a laudatory biography of his father-in-law, Agricola, who had been appointed governor of Britain, says that soon after the initial success of the invasion:

the nearest parts of Britain were gradually formed into a province, and in addition a colony of veterans was founded [at Camulodunum]. Certain tribal areas [civitates] were given to King Cogidumnus – he in fact remained totally loyal down to our times – in accordance with the Roman people's old and long-standing policy of making even kings their agents in enslaving peoples.

'Cogidumnus' is how the king's name is written in most of the extant manuscript texts, and it appears to closely match a name, the latter part of which survives on a dedicatory inscription found in Chichester early in the 18th century (Chapter 9). This fragmentary inscription refers to 'Ti[berius] Claud[ius] [?Co]gidubnus, [?great king or, less likely, king and imperial legate] in Britain', evidently the leader of a local people who had added two of the names of the illustrious Roman dynasty to his own, Celtic name. The name in the inscription and the name in Tacitus can be made to match each other with a change of one letter in the surviving text of Tacitus and restoring the first two uncertain letters of the name in the inscription to conform to those written in the text. This partly reconstructed name is the only written evidence to link Cogidubnus with Chichester or, indeed, anywhere else. The name does not appear on coins, a fact attributed to his not reigning

15

16

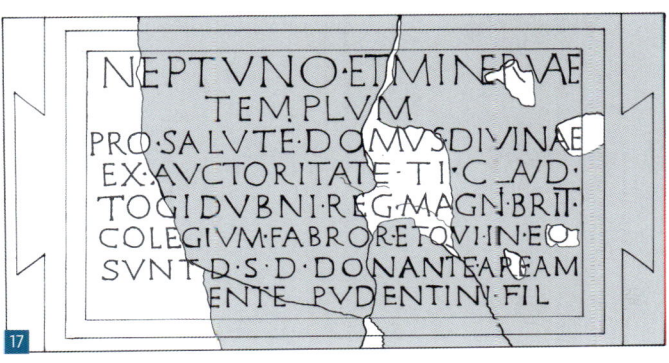

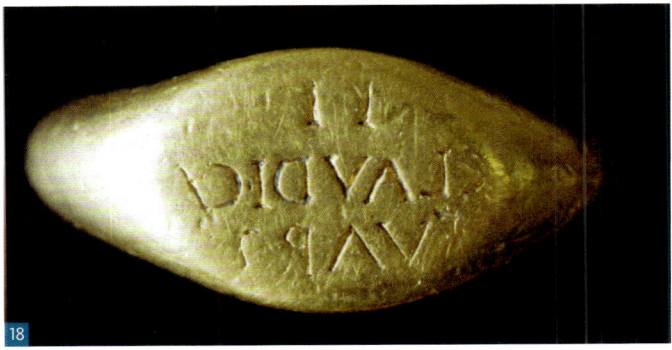

been assimilated to the Latin *regnum*, 'the kingdom'. The elaborate buildings at Fishbourne are reasonably interpreted as Togidubnus's own palatial residence and seat of government, in which case Togidubnus was paying tribute to Rome in more senses than one, for his obtaining the highest quality of classical architecture and decoration for Fishbourne suggests wholesale and conspicuous adoption of, and commitment to, Roman ways. Building Fishbourne would have entailed huge expense on his part, too, presumably paid for by local taxation as well as by the product of whatever estates were his own. While most other parts of southern Britain were placed directly under Roman law in a province ruled by a Roman governor, the Atrebatic kingdom of Togidubnus, like other client states, was privileged; people there were still able to carry weapons and they probably had to pay only the taxes due to their own king, determined according to their own rules and customs.

THE ROMAN TOWN

There is no definite evidence that a military base existed at Chichester or anywhere else nearby to protect the invasion-period supply depot at Fishbourne. Other supply depots situated in friendly territory did not have a fort near them. The existence of the highly Romanised palatial villa at Fishbourne, itself without obvious military protection, indicates that the territory was considered safe, with inhabitants likely to be well disposed to the Romans.

The archaeological evidence of the earliest buildings in Chichester suggests that these were constructed later than the period of the Roman invasion, and in any case they need not have had any military connection. The buildings were generally rectilinear, long and narrow in plan, end-on to the street, and made of clay and timber, with shallow foundations or no foundations at all. The materials and methods used are typical of the earliest buildings in many Roman towns in southern Britain, where such buildings could have had several functions, combining workshops with retail shops and houses, for example, passages at the side giving access to backyards. In those towns which definitely originated in a military base, there are differences between the initial military buildings and the succeeding buildings of the civilian town, and the buildings

before the Roman invasion as an independent king, and there are no other written references to him. Recent reconsideration of the name, prompted by the interpretation of another, similarly Romanised Celtic name on an inscribed gold signet ring excavated in 1997 in a 1st-century AD context at Fishbourne, suggests that the king is more likely to have been 'Togidubnus'. There are several Celtic analogues for such a name, whereas for 'Cogidubnus' there are none, and the inscription in Chichester can very reasonably be restored so as to read 'Togidubnus'.

Togidubnus ruled a client kingdom, that is, the Romans continued to allow him to rule his territory and people on condition that he maintained an alliance with Rome and paid whatever tribute was required. It is reasonable to suppose that he was the successor to Verica, the king of the Atrebates in alliance with Rome whose deposition was an ostensible reason for the Romans' invasion of Britain. Furthermore, as Tacitus says, other territories were added to his own, to form a sizeable client state apparently including the northern territory of the Atrebates with its centre at Calleva Atrebatum (Silchester) and a territory to the west, defined as belonging to another people, the Belgae, with its centre at Venta Belgarum (Winchester). The inhabitants of the original *civitas* of Togidubnus are documented as the Regni (or Regini), presumably a subset of the Atrebates, although their Celtic name seems to have

in Chichester resemble the latter more than they do the former. The dating evidence is not precise enough for us to be able to say exactly when these buildings were constructed, but any military base would have been of use only in the early stages of the invasion. Within one or two years the army had moved on, and was fully occupied, much further to the north and west.

Very early in the Roman period ditches were dug running from east to west, parallel to the east–west road of the town, and backfilled with earth containing pottery dated to before c AD 50. Later, a side street of the town was laid out along the same line. Pottery kilns existed at Rowlands Castle (Hampshire) and Dell Quay (Sussex), the former from before the Roman invasion and continuing afterwards, the latter not apparently in operation until much later, in the 2nd century AD. Fishbourne must have been supplied from elsewhere with the pottery vessels and other ceramic materials that a military depot would have needed. Pottery found at Chapel Street, in the north-west quarter of Roman Chichester, may have been early. A bathhouse in the same area contains flue tile in a form typical of the AD 50s and 60s rather than, say, the AD 70s and 80s.

The most precise evidence we have for the beginning of the town may be an inscription found in Chichester in the middle of the 18th century (and unfortunately soon lost, although its words were recorded). This was a dedication to Nero, datable to c AD 58–60, which may have been on the base of a statue or attached to a public building, possibly the large building of which traces have been found under the north side of East Street. The Togidubnus inscription in Chichester records the dedication of a temple to Neptune and Minerva by a college or guild of smiths. On epigraphic grounds alone, by the style of letter-cutting and the textual formulae used and without knowledge of Togidubnus, the inscription can be dated to roughly the third quarter of the 1st century AD. The dedication to the Roman god of the ocean and the goddess of skill and wisdom, respectively, has suggested a connection with boatbuilding. A temple need not have been urban. The apparently quite isolated temple on Hayling Island was rebuilt and continued in use at this time, but it was distinctly Celtic in form. By contrast, a temple to two divinities of the classical pantheon, and the existence of a college or guild of smiths

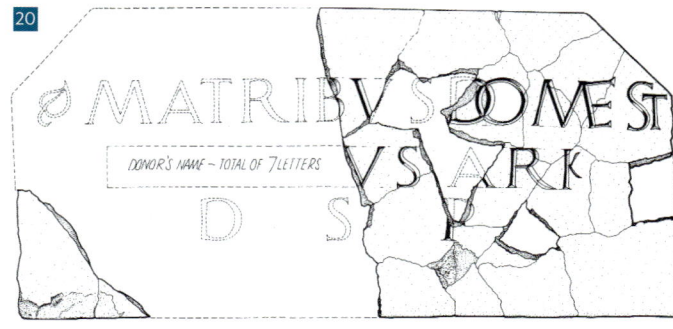

affluent enough to build such a temple, suggests an urban setting. Fragments of an inscription found in 1993 to the east of the Roman town, apparently a dedication to the *matres domesticae*, or 'mother goddesses of the home', is datable by style and form to the third quarter of the 1st century AD.

The name of the settlement is given by much later documents in rather garbled forms, clarified as 'Noviomagus Regnensium' or 'Noviomagus Regnorum' (or 'Reginorum'). The first element in this two-word name is Celtic in origin, as in the case of many town names in southern Britain, such as those of Calleva Atrebatum (Silchester), Venta Belgarum (Winchester) and Durovernum Cantiacorum (Canterbury), and can be translated in this case as meaning something like 'new place' or 'new market'. A similar Romano-British town name is that of Caesaromagus (Chelmsford, Essex), meaning something like 'Caesar's place' or 'Caesar's market' or, more exactly, a place or market town established by or in commemoration of Caesar. The second element of Chichester's Roman name, by analogy with other important towns, ought to refer to the name of the people of the surrounding *civitas*, who are documented as the Regni (or Regini), hence 'Regnorum' (or 'Reginorum'), meaning 'of the Regni' (or 'of the Regini'). This *civitas* was also known, in Latin, as simply *regnum*, 'the kingdom', so its inhabitants seem also to have been called, by extension, *regnenses*, 'people of the kingdom'. Contemporaries may have been as liable to be confused by this as we are now, all the more so since self-given ethnic names need not be very objective. The name of the Atrebates, for instance, apparently derives from a Celtic root meaning simply 'inhabitants'. In this case, the thoroughly Latinate

19 Roman coin depicting Nero

20 Reconstruction of a late 1st-century AD inscription to the household mother-goddesses; found at the Needlemakers, Chichester

21 Artist's reconstruction of Roman Chichester in c AD 125 (Mike Codd)

name of the Regnenses would suit a *civitas* that seems to have owed its autonomous existence to the collaborationist policy of a highly Romanised local Late Iron Age élite.

The *civitas* of the Regni would have wanted a town of the new Roman type in order to accommodate some of the economic activities now carried on in other such towns, whether or not these were previously functions of the Late Iron Age *oppidum* in the area. A town would not at first have been a necessary political centre of this *civitas*, however, as it was of other *civitates*. The government of the *civitas* of the Regni and the other parts of Togidubnus's client state would have been centred on Togidubnus himself, wherever he happened to be, together with his household, family or clan. Presumably he would usually have been at Fishbourne. The same could be said, incidentally, of the governor of the Roman province, the imperial legate, in whose person the government of the province, especially its military command, was concentrated wherever he was.

As Tacitus indicates, Togidubnus's client state was in Roman legal eyes a tributary state allied to Rome and technically outside the province of Britain, so the initiative in founding a town there would have belonged with the local ruler or, failing him, other local people acting with at least the king's permission and probably his patronage. For example, it would seem likely that the land on which the town was founded would have belonged to the king, or would have been in his gift. A town may actually have been a matter of pride for Togidubnus, because he seems to have been personally very much in sympathy with things Roman. The significance of the town's name may be that it was the new place or new market of the Regni, by contrast with the client state's other towns at Venta and Calleva, or in contradistinction to the former territorial *oppidum* in the area, or else perhaps because previously there had been nothing quite like it at all. In any case its initial purpose was probably economic, commercial and symbolic, as much as political.

Noviomagus would almost certainly have been founded in a deliberate act, for religious and legal reasons, and its first streets would probably have been laid out with appropriate care. A Roman surveyor setting out a military camp or a town or city on virgin ground would normally lay down the first road, the *cardo* or 'hinge' of the street plan, from south to north. This was the preferred primary axis probably because it was easy to establish from observation of the sun and shadows, and perhaps also because it was considered auspicious. It is possible that such an axis was set out running due north from the hypothetical intersection of land

surveyor's lines on the line of Stane Street (described above), or somewhere near it on this existing road line, and this was the main south–north road in the town (roughly on the line of modern North Street). Hitherto the principal axis of the town has been assumed to be the main east–west road (Margary 421), which John Magilton, writing in 2003, identified as the *cardo*. If the east–west road was already in existence it would have been convenient to make that the *cardo*, certainly. The main south–north road was also the main road from Calleva (Margary 155); this road, too, could have pre-dated the town, for the fact that it took a route running directly southwards as it approached Stane Street suggests only that it was carrying traffic likely to go south or west, not that this route was chosen in anticipation of, or after, the founding of the town. If the road was made at the same time as the town was founded, this would argue for the town's early date. If the road already existed it could have been redirected in order to be incorporated in the town's street grid, although excavations in 2006 north of the east gate in the Roman town, at the former Shippam's factory, found no evidence that a road had ever crossed the area obliquely from north-west to south-east (Chapter 10); only one road was found, running from west to east apparently parallel to, and north of, the main east–west road. As we do not know which of the two roads was laid out first, east–west (Margary 421) or south–north (Margary 155), we should call the south–north road the *cardo*, in accordance with normal Roman surveying practice. Other streets, known as *decumani*, would have been laid out crossing the *cardo* at right angles, with more streets parallel to the *cardo* at regular intervals to the west and east. The rectilinear grid of streets extending to the west and east of the *cardo* would thus demarcate, and give access to, blocks of land or *insulae*, 'islands'. The largest of the cross streets, known as the *decumanus maximus*, was usually in the centre of the grid. In Noviomagus, this cross street was made to coincide with the main road westwards, to Venta (Margary 421).

The street grid of Noviomagus extended over the area to the west of Stane Street and no streets seem to have been aligned to Stane Street itself. The strikingly cruciform layout of the four main streets of medieval and modern Chichester has misled many observers into thinking that these must necessarily follow the line of Roman streets. Three of them do, roughly, but South Street has been found to overlie Roman-period buildings, and its

---

22 **Early Roman Chichester – Noviomagus Reginorum (prior to 3rd century AD)**

precursor in Noviomagus would have been a little way to the east. The character of the central intersection of the main streets is uncertain; it is likely that these two streets did not simply cross as they do now, but one street may have been divided before it met the other, as in Londinium, Venta and elsewhere, to make way for important buildings. Stane Street may have continued, initially at least, to run uninterruptedly to a possible deep water anchorage and landing place at Copperas Point some 4km away to the south-west. Dell Quay, in shallower water further in Chichester harbour, was some 3km away, almost on the same road line. If goods had to be unloaded from large boats and ferried to shore

in small vessels it would probably have been worthwhile to land them at Dell Quay but, sea level being lower then, it's possible that Dell Quay was not navigable.

The limits of the town would probably have been marked or delineated in some way, but these limits need not have conformed to the later line of the walls. There is no evidence that the town was founded with walls (as will be explained) but, guarding against a circular argument, something can be deduced about the likely limits of the town by considering the line eventually taken by the walls in combination with the more direct evidence for streets,

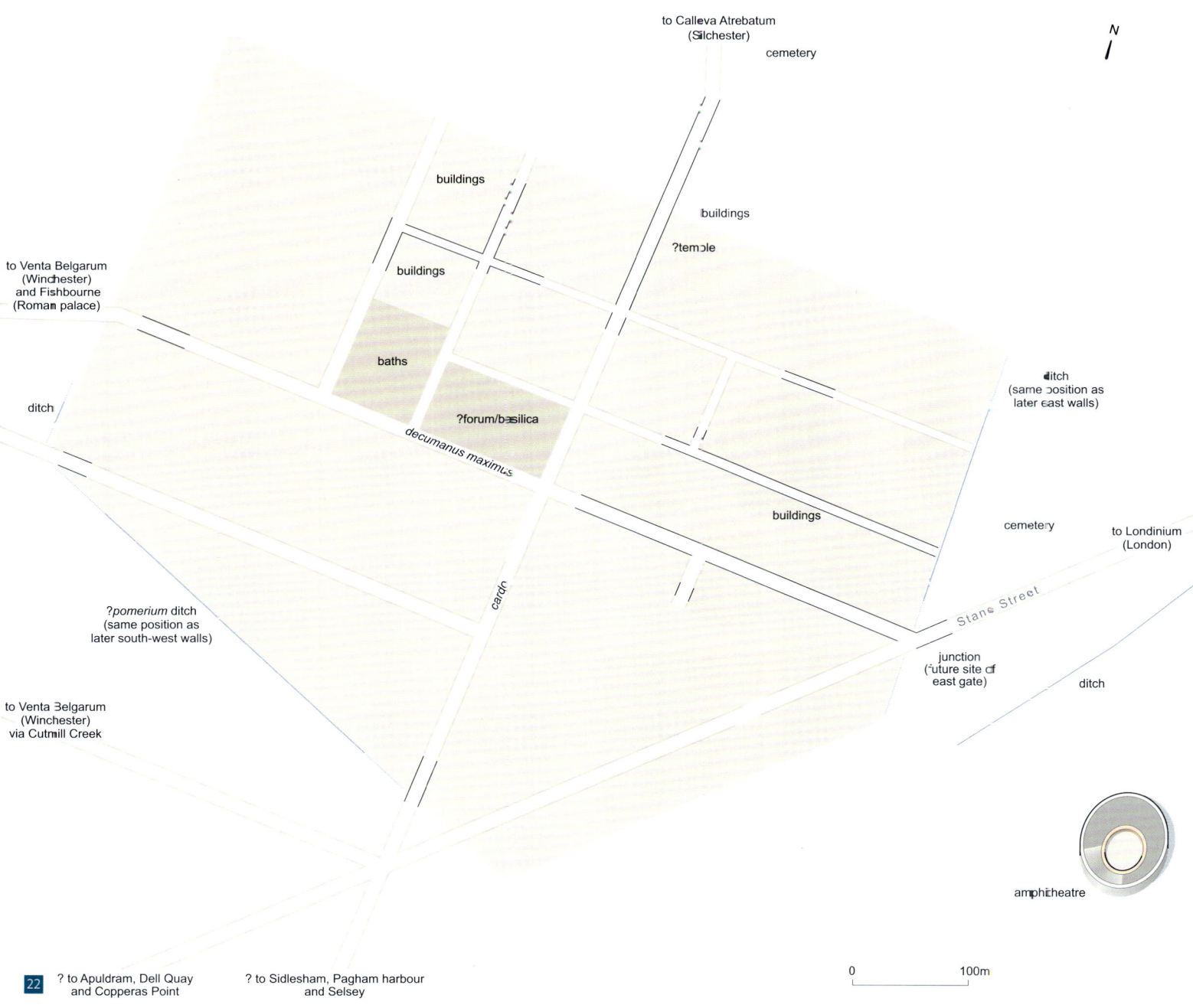

to Calleva Atrebatum
(Silchester)

cemetery

N

to Venta Belgarum
(Winchester)
and Fishbourne
(Roman palace)

buildings

buildings

buildings

?temple

ditch

baths

?forum/basilica

decumanus maximus

ditch
(same position as
later east walls)

buildings

cemetery

to Londinium
(London)

cardo

?pomerium ditch
(same position as
later south-west walls)

Stane Street

to Venta Belgarum
(Winchester)
via Cutmill Creek

junction
(future site of
east gate)

ditch

amphitheatre

? to Apuldram, Dell Quay
and Copperas Point

? to Sidlesham, Pagham harbour
and Selsey

0   100m

buildings and burials. There is evidence for buildings of various kinds being built at an early date beyond the later line of the walls, especially to the west, south and east. The northern road (Margary 155, described above) approached the town from the north-west and north, and its last change of direction may possibly coincide with the town limits on the north. Roman law and custom forbade burials, with very few exceptions such as neonates, within the limits of a town. The presence of burials just to the north, as well as to the east, at St Pancras on the north side of Stane Street, therefore implies limits to the town on those sides at least. A town of this kind would have had an area of countryside immediately around it (a *territorium*) serving for burials, water supply, possible expansion and so on. This land, too, could have been in Togidubnus's gift. There was no necessity in this early part of the Roman period to enclose a town in any more demonstrative way. The town limits could have been marked by a *pomerium*, or boundary ditch, especially if the town were founded and laid out as an expression of local royal policy. Some evidence was found in 2010 for a *pomerium* along the line later taken by the walls in their south-west and north-east quadrants, and the implications of this will be discussed in the context of the building of defences (Chapter 3). Towns and cities were the pre-eminent instrument and symbol of

civilisation, in Roman eyes, and the proof of civic peace was the open town, without walls or external barriers.

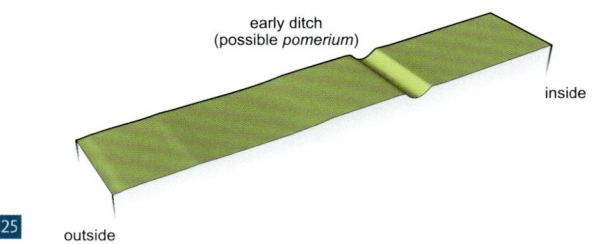

The other principal British client kingdom in alliance with Rome, beside Togidubnus's, was that of the Iceni, in East Anglia. Their experience is most instructive. The ruler of the Iceni died in AD 60 or 61 and the Roman province then, as expected, made to absorb the Iceni kingdom. Roman soldiers on police duty attempted to forcibly disarm the Iceni, which would have seemed a disgrace to a warrior aristocracy, and loans that had been made to the Iceni as a long-term investment were suddenly called in. The Romans' punitive response provoked the people and their royal leader, Boudicca, to revolt; her forces burnt the three nearest and most conspicuous towns newly planted after the Roman invasion, Camulodunum, Londinium and Verulamium (St Albans). The Roman army, in the face of this attack, had deliberately left these towns undefended, preferring to meet and defeat their enemy in the field which, on ground of their own choosing, they did. The Romans at this stage regarded their military machinery, which was essentially a mobile field army, as being very different from – and not to be encumbered by – the civil machinery of towns and town life. The rebellion must, however, have been a severe object lesson for those preparing for the eventual transition of Togidubnus's client state to the province.

To start with, Noviomagus was not the capital of a *civitas*, nor were Venta or Calleva, in so far as local government for all three territories was centred on the person of a single client king. These towns could easily take on the attributes of such a capital, however. In this respect they may be compared with the other nearby town, Durovernum, which was intended from the start to be the chief place of its *civitas*. Venta, Calleva and Durovernum were on the site of previous *oppida*. Main roads were built leading directly to them, and the junctions of these main roads were well inside the towns. If, by contrast, the founding of Noviomagus is regarded as later than, and secondary to, the construction of at least two of the main roads in the area, Stane Street and the road west running from it, and possibly a third, the south–north

road (as described above), its location can be interpreted as taking advantage of the junction of these roads. In much the same way the founding of Londinium, for instance, took advantage of a safe crossing of the River Thames in proximity to the head of an estuarial harbour. Like Noviomagus, Londinium was not founded as the capital of a *civitas* but within ten years (by the time of the Iceni revolt) it was, according to Tacitus, already a busy commercial centre; its geographical position in relation to the other towns, major routes and resources of Britain was such that it soon became the financial headquarters of the province in preference to Camulodunum. Noviomagus presumably became the capital of the *civitas* of the Regnenses only when the client kingdom was constitutionally absorbed into the province after Togidubnus's death. This date is not known but is unlikely, for reasons to do with Tacitus being our historical source, to have been later than AD 78.

Although numerous archaeological interventions and excavations have been carried out in the centre of Chichester, especially recently, their position and extent have been dictated by modern redevelopment and the plan of the Roman town can be recovered only gradually and piecemeal (it is estimated that not much more than 5% of the area of the Roman town has been excavated so far). As a town in Roman style, and especially once it had become the capital of a *civitas*, we can expect Noviomagus to have contained certain public buildings. At least one bathhouse has been found, in the north-west quarter of the town. In addition there would have been a forum, which was an open-air public square often surrounded by a colonnade and used as a market place. Invariably the forum was adjoined on one side by a basilica, which was a

large covered hall with numerous public functions, housing law courts, official records, tax collectors, local government functionaries and so on. In Britain forums were, for some reason, not associated with temples in classical form, which was the rule in Gaul and elsewhere. The plan of Noviomagus has been sufficiently excavated to suggest that its forum and basilica were on or close to the main east–west road and fairly central. These major buildings seem to have been built late in the 1st century AD.

The population of the town is difficult to estimate. An amphitheatre was built to the east of the town, about 200m beyond Stane Street, late in the 1st century AD, which may have held several thousand spectators, but they would have come from outside as well as inside the town. By the end of the 1st century AD, perhaps a generation or two after it was established, the town may have contained a few hundred households with a total population of 3000–4000 people. Although it is difficult to be sure, in size and character Noviomagus may not have changed much for several generations after that.

23 Beads, including ones made from amber and a dog's tooth, from a female burial at the St Pancras cemetery

24 2nd-century AD cremation and 3rd- or 4th-century inhumation burials in the cemetery at St Pancras

25 Schematic section through the possible boundary ditch

26 Goddesses on a fragment from the base of a Jupiter column that probably stood in the forum

26

3

Defending the Roman town: wall, gates and ditches

Roughly 200 years after Noviomagus, the Roman town of Chichester, was founded, walls were built enclosing the town. By 'walls' we mean a combination of an earth bank revetted on its outer face with a masonry wall, topped with a wall walk and parapet, and forming a defensible circuit around the town, together with a ditch or ditches beyond this circuit, gates admitting at least the main roads through the circuit, and possible ancillary structures such as gatehouses and towers. The archaeological evidence for the walls, so defined includes substantial upstancing remains of the bank and masonry wall themselves, but the evidence for other elements that were originally just as important, such as the gates and ditches, is not so obvious. The physical evidence for the walls has been investigated sufficiently up to the present moment for us to be able to propose a fairly coherent and plausible reconstruction of the walls and, furthermore, to imaginatively reconstruct the process by which they could have been built, in distinct stages. This may present an answer to the relatively straightforward questions: what were the walls and how were they built? However, it is not the only possible answer and will always be subject to interpretative disagreement as well as, of course, modification in the light of new evidence. The reconstruction will be described first, in a fairly narrative account, referring to the most relevant and important archaeological evidence (which is also presented in the gazetteer in chronological order of investigation in Chapter 10). The related questions of when the walls were built, by whom and why are inherently more difficult to answer, although historically vital. These aspects of the walls will be discussed subsequently. The process by which the archaeological evidence for Chichester's walls has been gradually recovered, increasing our knowledge of the walls, is itself inextricably a part of the history of the walls and is more fully described in Chapter 10.

SETTING OUT THE LINE OF THE WALLS

The aim of building walls around Noviomagus would presumably have been subject to tests of feasibility and economy. The existing town limits, or *pomerium*, would have provided a starting point for considering where the line of the walls should run. Often the *pomerium* of a town was marked by a boundary ditch, and sometimes by a gate or, even more elaborately, by an arch on a main road. In two places around Noviomagus, in the north-east and the south-west of the town, a relatively small ditch has been excavated which, from the fact that the walls were subsequently positioned directly on top of and more or less in line with it, may have marked the town's *pomerium*. Whether this was the *pomerium* is uncertain, for such a small ditch could have been dug simply to

set out the line of the walls, and even if it were initially the *pomerium* houses may have been built outside its line. In any event the actual line to be taken by the walls could have been decided quite pragmatically. The full extent of the urban settlement and its buildings was not, in itself, a crucial factor. Several buildings, including well-appointed houses furnished with mosaic or tessellated floors and walls faced with painted plaster, are known to have been demolished to make way for the walls and others were left outside the circuit. Even public buildings, such as the town's amphitheatre, could be left outside, too. Admittedly the amphitheatre may have fallen out of use by the time planning and construction of the walls began, although dating the end of its use is problematical.

In the event the line chosen for the walls enclosed a fairly compact area, seemingly taking in most of the side streets of the town and the buildings, or building plots, along them. Unfortunately we still know too little of the internal layout of the town and its streets to be sure, but on the available evidence it seems a reasonable supposition that the line of the walls would have respected as far as topographically feasible the existing arrangement of side streets and the plots of land, or *insulae*, between them. The line of

1   Detail from a mosaic floor of late 3rd- or 4th-century AD date from a building on the north side of East Street (David S Neal)

the walls was set out apparently respecting the existing street grid on both the east and west sides of the town, where the walls ran roughly perpendicularly to the *decumanus maximus*, the west–east axis of the town. The line of the walls on the east ran just to the east of the junction of Stane Street and the *decumanus maximus*. By crossing Stane Street just to the east of the junction, only a single gate in the walls would be required on this side of the town. If the gate could be shown to have been situated sufficiently to the west of the projected position of this junction, wholly on the *decumanus*, this would imply that Stane Street either no longer ran south-westwards from the junction, or was blocked by the walls.

On the opposite side of the town, to the west, the line of the walls crossed the *decumanus maximus* at a point that left the *cardo* nearly equidistant from the walls to its west, 390m away, and east, 380m. The *cardo* thus practically bisected the walled town, but it must be remembered that the street plan preceded the walls and that the walls, when they were being planned, could in principle have been placed almost anywhere. The fact that the line taken by the walls was nearly equidistant from the *cardo* suggests that

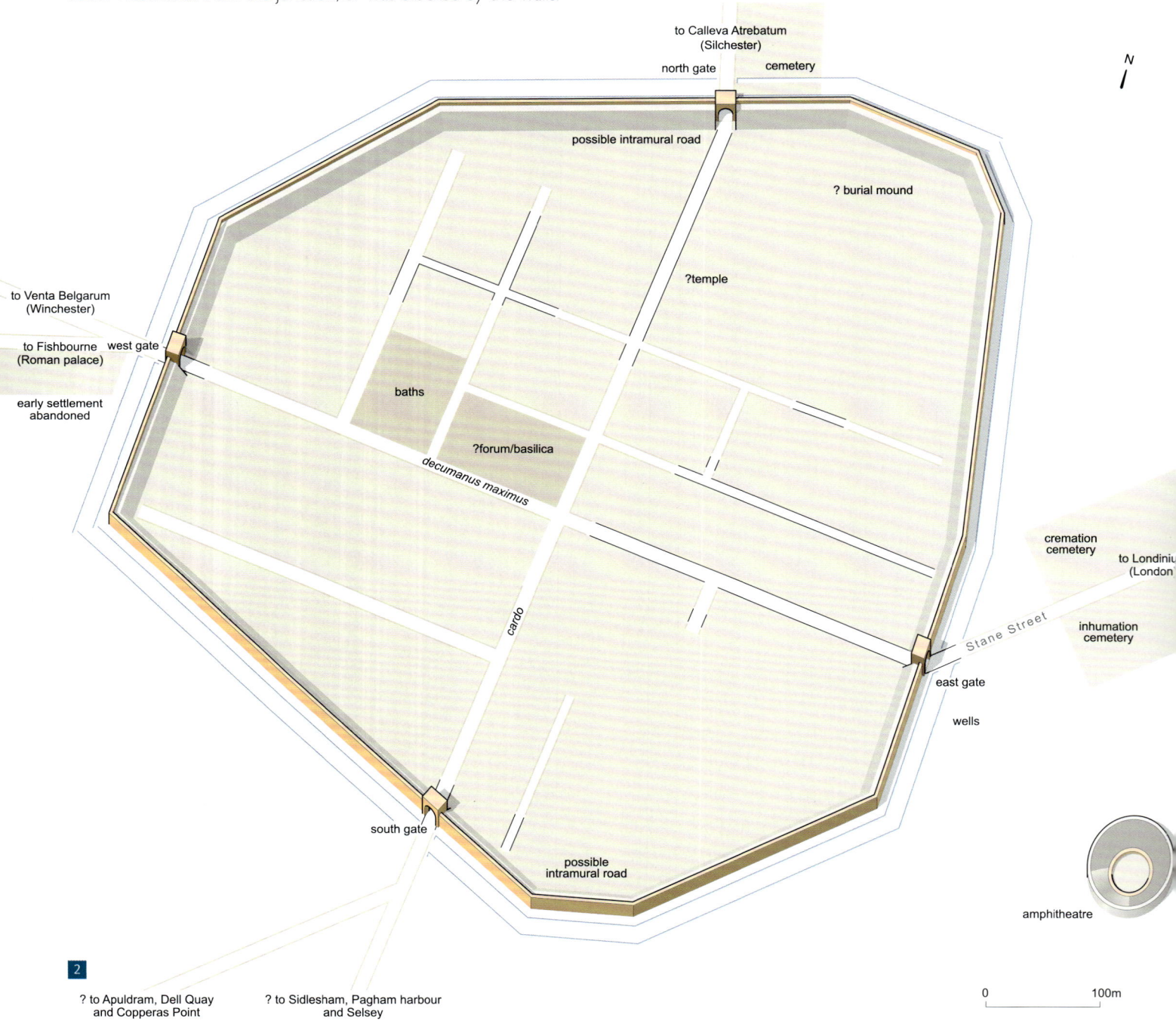

to Calleva Atrebatum
(Silchester)

north gate · cemetery

N

possible intramural road

? burial mound

?temple

to Venta Belgarum
(Winchester)

to Fishbourne   west gate
(Roman palace)

early settlement
abandoned

baths

?forum/basilica

decumanus maximus

cremation
cemetery

to Londiniu
(London

Stane Street

inhumation
cemetery

cardo

east gate

wells

south gate

possible
intramural road

amphitheatre

2

? to Apuldram, Dell Quay
and Copperas Point

? to Sidlesham, Pagham harbour
and Selsey

0   100m

this line may have followed the original town limits on the east and the west sides of the town. On the east side this conjecture is supported by the fact that a large, early cemetery was situated only a little further to the east, on the north side of Stane Street. On the west side a gate in the walls allowed the *decumanus maximus* to run through and then to continue, as it had before, further to the west, as the road to Venta (Winchester).

Evidence exists for side streets roughly parallel to either the *cardo* or the *decumanus maximus*, at least two in each case in the north-east and north-west quarters of the town. These street lines, if projected, would have subdivided the ground fairly regularly into rectangular *insulae*, each roughly 75m square or else roughly 75m from south to north and 90m from east to west. Although the grid thus formed by these street lines would not be exactly rectilinear the discrepancies of alignment are small enough, and of such a kind, that they can reasonably be attributed to imperfect land surveying. The line of the walls was made to run due north and south of the *decumanus maximus*, that is, north and south from the east and west gates, for a distance of about 110m, equivalent to roughly one and a half times the short (or north–south) side of an *insula*. From the four points thus reached by the line of the walls, the line began to close in on the south and north sides of the town.

On the south side, the south-east quarter of the town was enclosed by running the walls from north-east to south-west parallel to the presumed line of Stane Street and at a distance of about 80m from this road line, slightly more than the length of the short side of an *insula* elsewhere in the town. The south-west quarter was enclosed by running the walls from north-west to south-east to meet the line parallel to Stane Street at a point somewhat to the east of the line of Stane Street. The south gate in the Roman walls has been found to be a little to the east of the later, medieval south gate but, as we would expect, in line with the *cardo*. Although close, the Roman gate was situated a short distance to the north of the projected intersection of the *cardo* and Stane Street. It would have been more efficient, if Stane Street was in use as well as the *cardo*, to have run the walls a little further to the south so that a single gate could have closed Stane Street to the south of this projected intersection. There is no definite evidence one way or the other for another gate in the walls on the line of Stane Street, although it seems very

---

2 Roman Chichester, mid to late 3rd century AD

3 A side street running from west to east, revealed during excavations on the Shippam's site in the north-east quadrant

3

unlikely that there would have been another gate there so close to the known south gate. The implication (like the situation at the east gate) is that either Stane Street was not in use by this time or, when the walls were built, it was not given a gate and was blocked inside the walls. Oddly, the gate was not at the southern extremity of the circuit of the walls; the latter point was about 10m further to the south of the gate and 40m to the east, at a distance of about 270m from the *decumanus maximus*.

On the north side of the town the line of the walls was made to enclose the north-east quarter by running north-westwards at a fairly acute angle to a point some 370m from the *decumanus maximus*, the furthest from the centre of the town that the walls reached. The line then changed direction fairly sharply to the west and soon afterwards ran in a series of straight stretches to enclose the north-west quarter. A gate was built where the line crossed the *cardo* which, as before, continued to run further to the north as the road to Calleva (Silchester). The line of the walls in the north-east part of the town seems to follow a strangely circuitous route. There would seem to have been no strictly natural topographical reason for the line of the wall to take this course there, although very uneven terrain is a possible explanation. An alternative explanation is that this course was chosen in order to take in some existing feature in the north-east of the town and keep it within the enclosed area of the town. This possibility is strengthened by the fact that an extensive area of the Roman town excavated in 2006 on the north side of the *decumanus maximus*, just inside the east gate, seems not to have been built on very densely, if at all; the line of the walls seems to have been set out not to take in buildings in this area but rather, by implication, to take in something else further to the north. We have almost no clues as to what such a feature could have been. We may suppose that it was probably already in existence, and that it did not consist simply of otherwise ordinary houses, shops and workshops, since elsewhere, especially to the south and west, such buildings were demolished or left outside the circuit of the walls. The actual line taken by the walls suggests that the feature may have extended from west to east for at least 90m, equivalent to the long side of an *insula*. Obvious public institutions of importance, such as the forum and basilica, are known or reasonably inferred nearer the centre of the town, where they would normally have been. A substantial bathhouse is known in the north-west quarter of the town; possibly there was another to the north-east, although if so it would have been quite far away from the commercial centre and the majority of the town's inhabitants. The

town's already abundant water supply is unlikely to have required an aqueduct and *castellum*, or water tower and distribution centre which, if it had been needed, could have been this north-eastern feature. As already mentioned an amphitheatre, possibly disused, was left outside the walls. A theatre has recently been hypothesised elsewhere in the south-east quarter of the town, on the basis that its masonry remains may have determined or influenced the curved shape in plan of medieval streets forming West Pallant and East Pallant. The putative feature in the north-east of the town may have been a temple or structure of similar, non-utilitarian significance, although the later construction of a small medieval castle on the site (Chapter 6) suggests that this feature may simply have been a hillock of some kind which the castle reused. A hillock in the north-east of the town would have been too close for the line of the walls to have run to its south, leaving it just outside the walls, and it cannot have been feasible for some reason to reduce its height or remove it. Perhaps it was a large burial mound, like those thought to have been enclosed by the walls of Durovernum (Canterbury).

The ground surface in the Roman town seems to have been much less even, at least initially and in some places, than it was later (and is now). In at least one area in the town the initial ground surface seems to have been anomalously low, and was in due course infilled and levelled up. Elsewhere the ground had to be consolidated before the walls were constructed. Perhaps localised depressions such as this were the result of natural periglacial and postglacial thermokarsts (Chapter 2).

4

6

DIGGING DITCHES AND RAISING AN EARTH BANK

Once the line of the walls was determined, and therefore quantities of material and the likely costs could be calculated, the actual process of construction would probably have been undertaken in one stretch at a time, under appropriate supervision, so that construction proceeded slowly around the circuit. The process of construction apparently began with the demolition of any buildings in the way, the infilling of holes such as wells and the levelling up of uneven ground. The ground was cleared and obstacles reduced in this way where ditches were to run, as well as nearer to the town, where a bank and masonry wall were to be raised, as it would be important for the walls both to have a clear field of view in front of them and to be clearly visible. In at least two places a minor road was obliterated, and on the east side of the circuit a pre-existing ditch running roughly from north to south was filled in. As well as infilling wells and unwanted ditches the demolition debris was dumped to begin making an earth bank

along the line of the walls; the lowest stratigraphic position of this debris in the bank indicates that this material was dumped first, presumably being derived from the preparatory demolition.

The next task was to dig ditches, the upcast from which would also contribute to raising the earth bank. Along most or all of the line at least one ditch was dug at a distance of between 5m and 15m from the line to be taken by the bank, which was nearer the town. The ditches therefore did double duty, both providing material to form the bank and creating an obstacle in front of the upstanding element of the walls. The material in the bank

4 Roman oven, Shippam's site

5 Apsidal-ended hot room of the public bathhouse, Tower Street

6 A range of Roman cosmetic items found in Chichester – from top: bronze razor; bronze tweezers; bronze and silver hairpin; decorated bronze nail cleaner

conforms to that found in the subsoil of the area: generally gravel, brickearth and coombe rock. The ditches were typically about 5m wide or more and 2m deep, although subsequent weathering of the upper part of their sides has obliterated the original profile there. There is no evidence for a cleaning slot at the bottom of the ditches.

There is no evidence that earth was piled up high enough to make the bank defensible on its own, nor that it was provided with a timber palisade or timber revetment. Instead, we may assume that the outer face of the bank was intended to be revetted with a masonry wall. We do not know how high the bank was intended to be, nor whether the bank was intended to rise as far as the top of the masonry wall. The height of the bank would have depended very much on the materials, dimensions, form and functions of the wall. In at least one place, in the south-west quadrant, the earth of the bank was found to have been piled against the inner face of the masonry wall, perhaps because the wall was built away from the edge of the bank. The mechanics of transporting the upcast of the ditches implies, therefore, that material would have been carted around the unfinished end of the walls in the course of construction.

The fact that the ditches were on the outside of the circuit was an advantage in building the bank on the inside, since the ditches would be longer than the bank and thus yield a greater volume of material in proportion to the length of the bank. As the upcast would be dug up and become uncompacted, it would appear to produce a larger volume of material than the size of the ditches would have suggested, but the material in the bank would then have to have been left to be consolidated and become more compacted again before the bank was stable. There is no definite evidence that the exposed tail of the bank was systematically retained, using posts and boards, for instance, although this may have been done in places. As the material in the bank settled and weathered the slope of the bank could have spread somewhat. This would probably not have mattered, although in at least one place in the south-west quadrant the bank was revetted with a

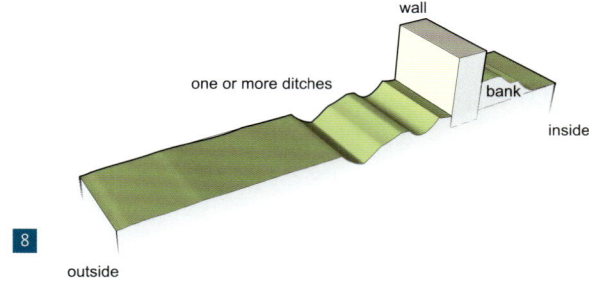

8

conforms to that found in the subsoil of the area: generally gravel,

low masonry wall, apparently to protect an intramural road and keep it clear. The growth of grass and other vegetation on the bank would have helped to consolidate it, and the evidence of possible turf lines in the remains of the bank has been taken to suggest its angle and therefore its height. Unfortunately such turf lines are not to be interpreted so simply. They could have been turves laid on the bank, or turf formed as the surface of the bank was allowed to develop vegetation, at an intermediate stage in its construction or at some much later time.

THE MASONRY WALL: DESIGN AND SPECIFICATIONS

The masonry element of the walls consisted of a wall on the outer face of the earth bank. Probably most if not all of the inner face of the wall was supported, and therefore hidden, by the bank while the outer face was exposed. Almost certainly the outer face of the wall rose to incorporate a parapet, which probably shielded a wall walk behind, running on top of the bulk of the wall, although no definite evidence for the top of the wall remains. The parapet was probably crenellated.

The maximum surviving height of the core of the wall is about 4.10m above present ground level; how much higher the wall was originally is not known. More surprisingly, only a single section has been cut through the full width of the wall in modern times to enable its original width to be directly seen and measured. This was in a tunnel through the wall to the north of the east gate, where the foundations were up to 3m wide and the masonry superstructure about 2.4m wide. The upper parts of the existing wall are not so old and superficial features, such as the modern footpath along the top of the wall, do not indicate its original width. In some places on the circuit the inner face of the wall has been shown to have been built with offsets, so this face was stepped back as it rose and the width of the wall at its base was broader than higher up, but in other places no such offsets have been found. The offsets may indicate contemporary variation in construction method, or subsequent rebuilding, or both. Unlike width, its height was naturally a very visible aspect of the wall. Whereas the width of the wall may have varied slightly according to local conditions and how the builders adapted themselves to these, its height would probably have been fairly uniform. The best estimate for the typical width of the wall is about 2.4–3.0m, and its height would have been related to, and limited by, its width for structural reasons. The highest known surviving portion of the original facing stones of the linear wall, at Friary Close in the south-east quadrant, is at a height of 1.70m above present ground level. The bulk of the wall would probably have been some 4.0m high up to the level of the wall walk, and this would have accounted for most of the mass of masonry. Above this level the parapet probably rose another 1.5–2.0m, with merlons projecting another 0.5m higher. The overall height of the wall from ground level on its outer face to the top of its merlons therefore may have been about 6.5m. The parapet and merlons would have been at least 300mm wide, leaving some 2.0m for the width of the wall walk, if this ran along only the top of the masonry. The wall walk could have been extended on its inner edge in timber, if necessary. There may have been steps at intervals up the bank to gain access to the wall walk from ground level in the town, and these could well have been of timber.

GATES

The circuit of the bank and wall included at least four gates, one on the east where the line of the walls crossed the existing Stane Street, one at the opposite end of the *decumanus maximus* where this became the road to the west to Fishbourne and Venta and, at two points on the *cardo*, on the north where this road then turned into the road going to Calleva and on the south where the road went to Selsey. The last, the south gate, controlled access between the town and its nearest harbours, at Copperas Point, Dell Quay and the eastern arm of Chichester harbour.

Some evidence has been seen for two of the original gates, at least, to indicate that they were flanked on one, if not both sides, by guard rooms and similar structures at ground level which, apparently projecting in plan on the inner side of the bank and wall, may have supported a more substantial structure at a higher level. There is no definite evidence, however, for the existence originally of gatehouses, much less towers, at the gates. Much later map views of Chichester from the 16th century onwards show the gates at the four cardinal points, with a gatehouse in each case, but these cannot be relied upon for detail. It is possible that at least some elements of the original, or early, gates survived until they were demolished in the late 18th century (Chapter 9). The southern jamb of the west gate is still *in situ*, incorporated in a corner of a later toll house, but whether this is part of the original structure is uncertain. The jamb consists of several well-squared

---

7 A section through the bank at the west side of the Bishop's Palace garden, looking towards the back of the masonry wall on the extreme right

8 Schematic section through the defences

and dressed blocks of sandstone, fitted to form a simple, squared pier. Its relative simplicity is attractive but does not argue in itself for a Roman date, as a stone gate pier of any later time is likely to have been equally simple in form. Samuel Hieronymus Grimm made a drawing of one of the gates which, if dating from 1782, can only have been of the east gate shortly before it was demolished (Chapter 9). The drawing depicts a wide round-headed arch over a wide thoroughfare, flanked by a narrower opening also with a round-headed arch, the latter opening for people on foot, both arches obviously built with large blocks of well-cut stone. Christopher Searle has persuasively identified the drawing as being of the outer face of the east gate, and says that the form of the gate suggests it could have been Roman. A medieval gate, built between, say, c 1200 and c 1550, would have been given a pointed arch; a gate could have been rebuilt later than c 1550, using a round-headed arch, which was a classical motif, but this is uncertain. It is unlikely that an earlier medieval gate built with a round-headed arch, before about 1200, would have been built well enough to survive. Small gates in similar form and of Roman date survive elsewhere, at Lincoln for instance.

The earliest seemingly accurate map of Chichester, William Gardner's map of 1769, shows the gates in plan, and they all seem quite simple. The only oddity is that the south gate is shown as being oblique to the general line of the wall, the line of the wall to the east being offset southwards with respect to the line to the west, but this gate belonged to a later period and the significance of this kink will be considered later (Chapter 5). The Roman south gate was some 10–15m further to the east.

The gates of Noviomagus are likely to have been fairly simple, consisting of a single gateway with possibly a pedestrian side gate as shown in Grimm's drawing of the east gate. The latter is likely to have been the most elaborate gate, as it straddled the main approach to the town from London (see discussion, below), but the other gates need not have been very different. If Grimm's drawing shows the form of the Roman east gate, then it was in fact not very elaborate, not for instance being a double gateway with two equally wide openings side by side. As well as separating the traffic going into and out of the town, if necessary, a central pier between the two openings of a double gateway could have supported a heavier superstructure. The absence of a double gateway implies a slighter superstructure, although a gatehouse of some kind would probably have existed. Remains have been found of the north and south gates, or rather of guard rooms

presumably next to these gates. These foundations comprised fairly massive, squared stone blocks, implying substantial structures. They were all re-entrant rooms on the inner side of the wall, and substantial walls may have been required there to retain the weight of the earth bank at their side and the tunnel over the roadway. The superstructure of a gatehouse above this level could conceivably have been of timber, but this is unlikely. There is no definite evidence for towers, whether over the gates or flanking them. In plan these gates would have been comparable to the simplest known Roman gates in the walls around Durovernum and Calleva, which seem to have been like short tunnels through a wall and bank, in contrast to other more elaborate gates built both at those towns and at Verulamium (St Albans).

It has not been possible yet to excavate where the course of the ditches and the line of the roads outside the walls intersect. Possibly the ditches were continuous in front of the gates, and

therefore the roads would have been carried over the ditches on short bridges, presumably of timber. The ditches may have been dug continuously in order to maximise the production of material for the bank, but this would have entailed the subsequent expense of building short road bridges and keeping them in repair. Very often ditches terminated to either side of a road line. Neither alternative would seem to confer a clear defensive advantage.

THE MASONRY WALL: MATERIALS AND METHOD OF CONSTRUCTION

The masonry wall is likely to have been constructed at the same time as a bank of earth was raised behind it. The bank supported at least the lower part of the wall and gave it added stability and robustness. The existence of the bank also gave added protection against the wall being rammed or undermined, if the town were ever besieged.

The wall was founded quite shallowly, with two or three courses of large flints laid in clay or gravel, rather than in mortar, forming the base of the wall immediately below contemporary ground level to a relative depth of 200–300mm. The wall was raised in stages or 'lifts', each about 0.5m high, the stones forming the outer face probably being laid first and then the core being roughly laid behind the face. The core has been found to be interspersed with thin layers of trampled earth at vertical intervals of roughly 0.5m, interpreted as evidence for a pause in construction at each of these levels. Pausing after each distinct 'lift' of a masonry wall was built would be normal practice. This evidence for successive lifts has been recognised in transverse section across the width of the wall and in elevation along the face of the wall, where the original core has been exposed, and has been taken to be a distinguishing mark of the original wall core. Not enough of the core has been exposed in a single section or elevation, however, to be able to systematically investigate the horizontal extent of these lifts and determine how different builds may have been connected along the length of the wall. At any one time labour and the supply of materials would probably have had to be concentrated in only one place, or at most two places. There may have been as many as eight lifts in the main core of the wall, if this was 4.0m high, so a stretch of wall that was actually under construction would

9 The southern jamb of the west gate is still visible

10 The back of the wall, on shallow foundations, in the Bishop's Palace garden

39

probably have appeared as a stepped series of lifts, progressively rising from ground level. Perhaps the open ends of each lift, where construction was to continue, were retained temporarily with earth or timber shores while the mortar hardened sufficiently for construction to proceed further.

The outer face was almost certainly raised in stages corresponding to the lifts visible in the core. Very little of the original or of any early face survives intact; only a few patches are likely still to be *in situ* in places where a bastion or tower was later added, protecting the face (Chapter 4). Where a face seems to be original, or at least early, it consists of relatively small, roughly squared blocks of stone laid to regular courses in hard lime mortar. The courses are smaller and more regular than those of the core, which would have assisted adhesion to the core. The mortar in the face is harder than that in the core and in places has been identified as containing ground ceramic, serving as a better binding aggregate and giving the mortar a pink colour. The size of stones and type of coursing qualifies for the contemporary term *opus quadratum*, also sometimes called by archaeologists *petit appareil*, in contrast to masonry that consisted of much larger ashlar blocks. It is possible that the wall face was itself rendered with mortar and that this render was painted; it would have been possible to limewash the surface and paint lines to evoke the much thicker courses of ashlar masonry typical of *grand appareil*. There is no definite evidence for this here, although it is attested elsewhere. The face could have been rendered and limewashed without being subsequently painted to resemble ashlar.

The outer face was not necessarily founded on footings or a plinth course, and there may have been a slight batter to this face as it rose. The level of the wall walk, and the base of the parapet, may have been marked by a string course of larger blocks of stone, partly decorative, partly to shed water away from the face below and partly to give the parapet a firmer base. The top of the parapet and the merlons would have been capped specially in order to throw off water. Long capstones, moulded to be triangular in section with their apex upwards, are known from other Roman town walls and have been found *ex situ*, even where the walls do not survive to their original full height, as in London. No such stones have yet been identified from the walls of Noviomagus. There is implied evidence for drainage through the wall, as might be expected in such a watery place; a stone-revetted culvert running across the bank, recorded in the south-east quadrant, presumably continued originally through the masonry wall.

The stone used in the outer face seems to have been generally malm stone, a friable, hard form of chalk in the Upper Greensand. The nearest sources may have been at Cocking, 12km to the north, and possibly Amberley (both in Sussex), 17km to the east. Other suitable stones from nearby may have been used, such as stone from Lavant (Sussex), 3km to the north of the town. The main consideration would have been the ease of quarrying the stone and especially how easy it would have been to transport from the quarry to the site. Quarries on the seashore, such as a possible quarry at Mixen Rock, now offshore, or even at Quarr (Hampshire) on the north-east shore of the Isle of Wight, would have loaded their product on to boats for transport along the coast. In general it was compellingly cheaper to transport heavy materials such as building stone, in bulk, by sea or river than by land for any distance greater than about 12–15km.

The core of the masonry wall was raised in successive lifts, immediately after the outer facing stones were laid in each lift. The core consists of flints laid roughly to courses with abundant white or mid yellow, moderately hard, sandy lime mortar, the courses of flints being generally 100mm or more in height. The character of the Roman wall core is well demonstrated by its inner face at a low level, where it was not intended to be exposed, and recorded, for instance, in excavations in 1987–8 in the south-west quadrant; in the south-east quadrant the core has been described as containing large flints in regular courses with thick layers of mortar.

The courses of flints in the core appear to have been laid from at least one face, rather than simply tipped from above, for which purpose close access would have been necessary. Putlog holes detected occasionally in the core may be evidence for scaffolding erected against the outer face, afterwards removed, or the core could have been laid from the bank as both rose in height. We do not know if the earth bank was raised to its full height before, during or after construction of the core, nor what its full height eventually was. However, some of the irregularities seen in the outer face of the bank, which were at first interpreted as cutting back the bank in order to add the masonry wall, may have been openings made locally to gain access to enable the inner face of the core to be built free-standing. Equally, these irregularities could

---

11 A portion of original outer facing of the wall survives behind the site of a bastion at Friary Close

have resulted from exposing the inner face of the core at a slightly later time in order to be able to make repairs to the wall.

Mortar was at least as important an ingredient in the masonry wall as flint and other stone. The mortar would have been made from chalk, probably obtained from the Downs, although a nearer outcrop of chalk is at the Broyle, only 4km to the north of the Roman town, where chalk was quarried for mortar in the 18th century (leaving a large quarry about 200m square and 12m deep). The chalk, in suitable lumps, was first burned in a kiln to form quicklime (ie calcium carbonate is converted to calcium oxide by driving off carbon dioxide). A certain amount of water would be added to the quicklime, slaking it (giving off heat and forming calcium hydroxide). The resulting lime putty would be best thoroughly mixed and then left for some time, possibly for weeks or months and sometimes under water, before being knocked up or agitated and made more liquid again and mixed with an aggregate such as sand, usually in the proportion of one part lime putty to two or three parts sand, ready for use. From this point lime mortar begins to set in earnest, but only slowly by reacting with the atmosphere (absorbing carbon dioxide to go back to calcium carbonate). It may have been necessary to carefully control the rate at which the mortar in a lift of masonry dried out by keeping it damp at first; initial setting could take several days, but the resulting mortar would become harder still with the passage of time. Sometimes a pozzolan was added to the putty, typically finely crushed brick or tile, giving the mortar a pink colour. (Pozzolan, originally volcanic ash from Pozzuoli near Naples (Italy), contains vitreous silica that reacts with calcium hydroxide to produce calcium silicate, a kind of cement, and this property is shared by the silica in finely crushed ceramics.) The added pozzolan has the effect of making lime mortar set hard in the presence of water (ie it becomes a hydraulic mortar), increasing its resistance to weathering and its compressive strength.

DISCUSSION

The best evidence for date obtained so far suggests that the walls of Noviomagus began to be constructed at some time in the second half of the 3rd century AD, when the town had already been in existence for around 200 years. For most of that time Noviomagus had been, as it was to remain, the chief town of the *civitas* of the Regni. The walls themselves provide almost no intrinsic evidence for their date, other than the fact that their materials and method of construction are Roman in character, the nearest well-attested parallels being the walls of Venta, Calleva and Durovernum. The first two towns were given walls, first of earth and later of masonry, relatively soon in their life, and much early archaeological effort went into investigating whether the walls of Noviomagus were not constructed in this way, too. It used to be generally accepted that Romano-British towns were fortified in two stages, firstly with earthen ramparts and secondly, perhaps when these ramparts proved insufficient or more resources became available, with stone walls, usually revetting the existing earthen ramparts. That the earth bank at Noviomagus had functioned for a while as a defensive structure, without a masonry wall, was once thought to be likely, by analogy with other towns such as Venta and Calleva. Earthen ramparts were built relatively early in the life of these towns, so the question is partly one of date; such earthen ramparts are not characteristic of later town defences. The walls of Durovernum may be a better parallel to those at Noviomagus, being built of masonry backed by an earth bank in a single phase of work, and their construction is similarly now dated to about the end of the 3rd century AD. By that time backing a masonry wall with an earth bank may have been old-fashioned, but it allowed for economy of materials, especially where stone or tiles were in short supply. The masonry wall at Noviomagus was built without periodic levelling courses of tiles, such as were commonly inserted in mass stone masonry of this kind from

perhaps the 2nd century AD onwards. In this respect also it is like the walls of Durovernum as well as those of the Saxon shore fort at Dubris (Dover, Kent), of about the same date (discussed further, below).

John Magilton discussed in 1993 the latest evidence for dating the construction of the walls, as described above, drawing particularly on evidence found in recent excavations in the south-west quadrant. Previously the received view had been that the ditches and bank, followed by the masonry wall, represented two distinct phases of construction both to be dated to late in the 2nd century AD, but this date was based on very little datable material, notably relying on imported finewares such as samian with closely determined dates of introduction. Excavations necessitated by storm damage in 1987 presented an opportunity to gather more information, and especially to examine coarsewares which, though much more abundant than the imported finewares, had not been properly examined hitherto. Locally made coarsewares were now capable of being assigned date ranges, with likely dates of disuse as well as of introduction (dates of disuse being less easily applicable to finewares). Before the walls were built a building had existed on this site and was then demolished, presumably prematurely to make way for the walls. This building was probably constructed and could have been demolished early in the 3rd century AD. The earth dumped to form the bank directly on top of the demolished building contained coarsewares datable to the later 3rd century AD, and logic would suggest that a long interval of time would not have elapsed between demolition of the building and construction of the walls. The latest layers of the bank contained coarsewares of later 3rd- to mid 4th-century AD date and a late 4th-century AD coin. If these objects are not interpreted as intrusive, the context in which they were found may have been either rubbish and similar material accumulated during the life of the walls or else possibly the result of a later repair. There is evidence elsewhere within the bank and the masonry wall for the subsequent repair and rebuilding of the latter, and in any case there was a major reinforcement of the walls later on in the Roman period (Chapter 4).

12 There is remarkably little military evidence comtemporary with the wall, although much (as in the rest of Britain) dating to the 1st century AD – from left: segment of bronze lorica neck armour; lump of chain mail; bronze shield boss

13 Imported and locally made pottery, from a 2nd-century AD burial at St Pancras

13

The walls of Noviomagus were intended to be built of masonry from the beginning. If to start with only an earth bank was wanted, this might well have been curved. The line of the walls in fact comprises a series of straight stretches with relatively well-defined changes of direction, especially noticeable at the extreme northern and southern limits of the circuit, where the shortest straight stretches in the circuit round off corners. This suggests that the line was set out in the expectation of building a masonry structure, rather than simply an earth bank. As stated, there is no evidence for any fortification of the bank before the masonry wall was added.

The ditches would in due course have had a defensive function, but their number, length and size were determined in the first place by the need for material with which to make the bank. Transporting worked stone was expensive enough, and any material obtainable more locally, or even on the spot, would have been preferred. Although exact quantities are difficult to establish, as so many working assumptions have to be made, it is worth calculating at least an approximation of the quantities of material that the walls required. The length of the masonry wall along its outer face was (and is) c 2375m, and the following calculations assume a simple linear construction, ignoring the gates and the fact that the ditches on the outside of the circuit were longer than the bank and masonry wall on the inside. Assuming that the bank reached the top of the wall walk, a height of 4m, and was at least 10m wide with a simple triangular section, its volume would amount to 47,500m³. The volume of a single ditch 5m wide and 2m deep would be 11,875m³, and two such ditches would correspond to less than half the volume of the bank. If the ditches were the main source of material for the bank, we could conclude from this calculation alone that the bank did not rise as high as 4m; without allowing for compaction and assuming the same angle of repose of the material in the bank, half the volume would produce a bank less than 3m high. The flint and mortar core, if 3m wide and 4m high, would amount to 28,500m³. The proportion of solid flint in the core is difficult to ascertain, but it may have been about 70%, that is just under 20,000m³. The mortar would presumably have been derived from chalk, and both the flint and the chalk would have been quarried and transported together from the Downs, for a distance of at least 5km and, to be economical, not more than 15km. The stone for the face would have been dressed at the quarry to minimise the amount needing to be carried, and once dressed, and assuming that the parapet was some 330mm wide, this stone could have amounted to some 5350m³.

To illustrate the mechanics of overland transport of the material needed to build the masonry wall, we may assume that the stone and chalk weighed about 1.5 metric tons or tonne (1 metric ton equals 1000kg) per cubic metre and that donkeys were the means of transport, each weighing 150kg and capable of carrying 20% of its body weight in a pair of panniers slung across its back. On this basis we can estimate that to transport the flint (weighing 29,925 tonnes) would have required a total of nearly 1 million donkey-loads, the chalk for the mortar (12,825 tonnes) some 427,500 donkey-loads and the face stones (8025 tonnes) some 267,500 donkey-loads. During the colder winter months, as well as on very rainy days, mortar would not have set and the work would have ceased, therefore. At a guess the work may have carried on for 150 days in the year. For the sake of example we may imagine, say, 200 donkeys making one laden journey from the quarry to the construction site and returning unladen every day, at which rate transporting all the material would take more than 56 years. A donkey can pull twice its own weight in a cart, but carts may have been scarcer than donkeys and would have required maintenance and repair, just as animals require feeding and watering. If we imagine 20 carts, each pulled by two donkeys, making one return journey a day, this method of transport would take more than 28 years to move all the material. A combination of, say, 200 pack animals and 40 draught animals could move everything in less than 20 years.

These calculations are purely illustrative. They are intended to convey an impression of how much work was entailed in the construction of the walls. It would be easy, as passing observers at some long remove in time, to ignore this aspect of the walls and take their existence completely for granted, rather as if they had emerged into the light of day entirely of their own accord (a fallacy of reifying the objects and features they discover to which archaeologists are

14

sometimes liable). The many assumptions in these calculations are of different kinds, those to do with the strength of a donkey being perhaps less variable than those to do with the distance they had to plod. For instance, perhaps the chalk and flint could be found near enough for two laden journeys to be feasible per day, or perhaps oxen could be used instead of donkeys, ox carts moving much more slowly but having much more than twice the carrying capacity. In either case the time required overall could easily be halved. By contrast, the size of the human labour force and how long they took to do their work would have depended on organisation, skills and many other factors even less amenable to calculation than donkeys and oxen. A large number of labourers would probably have been required, as well as a few workers with specialist skills in mixing mortar and facing up a wall, all of them being supervised by one or more surveyors. We do not know if these workers were slaves, soldiers, impressed labour or free men receiving wages. As an aside, a late Roman writer noted that skilled builders were sent from Britain to Gaul at the end of the 3rd century AD to repair damage to a city's walls, so experienced builders certainly existed. There may have been an abundance of such builders in Britain then, at least by comparison with Gaul; the date is roughly when several British towns were having walls constructed, or recently had them constructed, including Noviomagus.

It is clear that encircling Noviomagus with walls was a very substantial and, no doubt, expensive construction project. Who undertook it and paid for it, and why? We do not know for certain, but in most circumstances it is likely that the *civitas* of the Regni would have been responsible, both for initiating and for implementing the work. Since the death of their last tribal ruler, Togidubnus, and the incorporation of the *civitas* in the Roman province of Britain some 200 years before, the Regni were probably still governed, at least at a local level, by an oligarchical landowning social elite, the descendants of a tribal aristocracy. According to Roman rules perfected in the administration of the provinces of Gaul in the 1st centuries BC and AD, the Regni formed a *civitas peregrina*, defined as a local state of non-Roman citizens (*peregrini*) largely responsible for their own affairs provided that they kept the peace, paid their taxes and submitted to Roman law as and when required. Although many variations are known, the constitution of such a state would roughly follow the model of provincial settlements of Roman citizens, *colcniae*, where

Roman law prevailed, as well as of Rome itself. Within a *colonia* the highest authority was the *ordo* of *decuriones*, nominally 100 in number and corporately constituting a *curia* or council. To belong to the *ordo* one had to be male, free-born, at least 30 years old and own a substantial amount of property. The *curia* annually elected two magistrates, *duoviri*, who presided over the *ordo* and tried minor criminal and civil cases, and two *aediles*, more junior officers responsible for such things as roads, drains and the water supply. A lesser state such as the *civitas peregrina* of the Regni would have had similar arrangements, although tribal laws and custom may also have been observed. The *curia* could have met anywhere, but prestige and convenience ensured that usually it met in a basilica in the chief town of the *civitas*, and we would expect such a seat of local government to have existed in Noviomagus.

The most relevant aspect of this system of public life was the prevailing culture of private munificence for public ends, allied with patron-client relationships. Most public institutions and public buildings in the Roman world were provided by individual benefactors or by subscription. Local revenue in a *civitas* came from renting out land and buildings, from tolls on goods brought to market, from penal fines, from the customers of municipal bathhouses and, if applicable, from selling water from aqueducts. The main taxes imposed were an annual poll tax and a land tax, from which Roman citizens were exempt (they paid an inheritance tax and obligatory fees). The revenue thus raised went mainly to pay for the army, which also had crude law enforcement functions. Every five years the magistrates of a *civitas* had extra responsibilities, especially to reassess liability for tax, sometimes by means of a census. The conclusion must be that the main contributors to meeting the cost of any town walls would have been the members of the *ordo* themselves, and theirs would normally have been the decision to apply for permission to build the walls.

14 Roman glass vessels from burials at St Pancras
15 Two sections of ceramic water pipe from Fishbourne

15

The members of the *curia* of the *civitas*, known later as *curiales*, were supposed to live if not in the chief town then at least within the territory of their *civitas*. At least one of the houses demolished to make way for the walls of Noviomagus, in the south-west quarter, seems to have been almost luxurious and a fitting residence for a *curialis*. One may wonder how influential the owner of such a well-appointed house could have been if the house were thus demolished, but it is possible that the owner had no choice. The owner (not necessarily the same person as the occupier) may have had other, better houses anyway, and perhaps handsome compensation was forthcoming for the demolition.

How could these local people afford to build walls? What resources and industry supported the local economy, and provided the wherewithal for such a construction project as the walls of Noviomagus? Could privately financed public munificence (which modern historians call euergetism) alone finance such a project? Were the building materials compulsorily purchased or requisitioned? Strabo's much-quoted list of products for which Britain was known to the Roman world (Chapter 2) is important, simply because so little literary attention was paid to such matters. We know that in a later period iron from the Weald of Kent and Sussex was important to the army, which included the transport and other ships of the *classis Britannica*, the British Fleet, based on both sides of the Strait of Dover. Grain is documented as having been shipped from Britain to supply the army on the Continent throughout the Roman period. Wool and woollen cloth were also notable products. Specific kinds of British cloth, including high-quality cloaks, were documented towards the end of the 3rd century AD (in the Emperor Diocletian's edict of prices). Noviomagus would have been one of the places where such goods as these were brought for sale, and we can guess that local products would probably have included cattle, salt, iron, grain and wool. Salterns are known around Chichester harbour and salt was, among other things, a vital ingredient in tanning hides. Although some local salterns may have gone out of use at the end of the 2nd century

AD, it is unlikely that the local market for salt ended. Other goods, such as iron and timber from the Weald, could have been trans-shipped through Noviomagus. The ready availability of wood for charcoal allowed the iron ore to be smelted where it was found, and only the metal was transported to market in the form of billets; some may have been transported, probably by coastal boats rather than overland, to concentrations of smithing workshops in north Kent and on the south side of London, for instance. Sheep and cattle could have grazed the thinner and poorer local soils, which were less suitable for agriculture; alluvial gley soils that dry out in summer, and saltings on the coast, would have provided summer grazing. Bones constitute archaeological evidence for the animals, and spindle whorls for weaving. Other local products may have included shellfish. The tidal coastal shallows of Chichester harbour and Selsey would have been a suitable habitat for oysters, and the ubiquity of Roman-period oyster shells in archaeological excavations attests to the efficiency of their production and transport. It would have been these resources that would have provided the wealth for local inhabitants, especially *curiales*, to be able to afford to build town walls. The suspicion remains, however, that the project may have been made feasible only by compulsory purchase of materials, perhaps at a discount, and compulsory labour, similarly for little remuneration beyond board and lodging (the latter resembling impressment in the 17th century; Chapter 8).

According to Roman law, a civilian could not carry a weapon without imperial permission. In the same spirit a town or city could not build itself defences without imperial permission. This was partly because emperors and governors were naturally concerned not to allow many towns and cities thus to create strongholds that could, in the wrong circumstances, be held against them by possible rival forces. Such approval was partly necessary to sanction any extra local taxes or imposts to pay for building walls (comparable to murage in medieval England; Chapter 7). Emperors may have publicly complained at the extravagance of towns and cities spending too much on such things as walls, but this complaint sounds like a politic pretext for refusing permission or deterring applications for permission. We do not know the reasons for which towns in Britain obtained approval for their respective walls.

16 **Richly coloured painted wall plaster from a Roman villa at Chilgrove, 8.5km north of Chichester**

17 **4th-century AD mosaic floor from Chilgrove, which gives an indication of the wealth of the area**

To secure political advantage a *civitas* or town could obtain an avowed patron, someone who would use their influence with higher authority on the town's behalf, though none is recorded from Britain. The historical context may explain the decision in the case of Noviomagus.

Between the foundation of Noviomagus and the time, probably 200 years later, when a decision was made to build walls around the town and the necessary approval was received, huge changes had occurred in the political and cultural character of the Roman world. Britain, which had not been completely subdued in the north, contained in consequence a disproportionately large garrison and was the focus of intermittent military campaigns. Imperial power depended on the loyalty of the army. When an emperor proved to be incompetent, the succession

18

seemed uncertain or army officers in highly militarised provinces such as Britain were overambitious, the army had proved to be the major political player, but a divided army raised the risk of civil war. Usurpers tried to buy their soldiers' loyalty by increasing pay, setting up their own mints, if necessary, and debasing the coinage to make the specie or precious metal in it go further. Suspicious of the potential danger of rebellion in large provincial garrisons, certain provinces were split up; early in the 3rd century AD Britain, for instance, was divided into two provinces, with their respective capitals at London and York, and later these were subdivided again. In AD 193 armies in three different provinces proclaimed their respective commanders as emperor, one being Clodius Albinus, based in Britain. After he was defeated in Gaul and killed in AD 196 the victor, Septimius Severus, imposed a punitive reaction in Britain. Severus later arrived in person, with his entire court, to lead a campaign against resistant peoples in the north of Scotland, but after limited success fell ill and died at York in AD 211. The social origin of senior officers and bureaucrats was no longer the aristocratic senate, but included men who rose

from the ranks. A kind of militarised bureaucracy grew up, its members carrying out civilian administration but with military ranks and uniforms. Early in the 3rd century AD a radical legal change, the extension of Roman citizenship to almost all the free inhabitants of the empire, was probably accompanied remuneratively by an end to the exemption of citizens from the poll tax and land tax. The social and legal basis of membership of the Roman world was shifting. In the middle decades of the 3rd century AD advantage was taken of external incursions and unrest to set up a separate empire in Gaul, shortly extended to Britain and eventually defeated in AD 274. Economic decay led by inflation over a period of decades was matched by political and military chaos.

Within a few years, in AD 283, control of the forces in Britain and Gaul was taken by Carausius, who had been in command of naval forces in the English Channel, which were based at Boulogne as well as at forts and harbours along the south-east coast of Britain. The purpose of these forces and their bases, set up earlier in the 3rd century AD and known in contemporary and later documents as the *litus Saxonicus*, or Saxon shore, was mainly the suppression of piracy and seaborne raiding by people from beyond the empire's boundaries. The nearest forts in this system to Noviomagus were at Portchester (Hampshire), to the west, and Pevensey (Sussex), to the east, while Dover and Canterbury, as mentioned, were also fortified. Carausius presented himself as a commander whose claim to regional rule was at least as strong as that of the other rulers in a new arrangement by which the Emperor Diocletian delegated some of his authority to a co-emperor, Maximian. Diocletian was the senior man and emperor in the east, while Maximian was emperor in the west, where he had previously been Carausius's superior. Each took the title of 'Augustus', and conferred the title of 'Caesar' on a junior colleague who, it was expected, would succeed him; the four nominally joint rulers formed a tetrarchy. Events are documented by unreliable panegyrists, but it seems that Maximian's Caesar, Constantius, audaciously captured Boulogne in AD 289, whereupon Carausius was murdered and supplanted by one of his erstwhile lieutenants, Allectus, who then retreated to his presumed military base in Britain.

Constantius, to restore legitimate rule and his own standing, had to mount an invasion of Britain in more daunting circumstances than those faced by the Emperor Claudius or by Julius Caesar in earlier days, for he was opposed by Roman forces like his own. By the time Constantius launched this invasion in AD 296,

Allectus would have been able to continue and even complete works of fortification that had probably been begun by Carausius, such as building a wall along the north bank of the River Thames, together with storehouses and similar installations, to complete the defences of London. Constantius, trying to land his forces in two places, took the short crossing from Boulogne to east Kent but did not make landfall. His general, Asclepiodotus sailing from the mouth of the Seine and managing under cover of fog to evade a naval ambush in the Solent, landed probably somewhere near Portchester. Allectus, who had been preparing to repel Constantius in Kent, moved his forces inland to meet Asclepiodotus's army. For whatever reason, perhaps because his forces were gathered in haste, were unused to fighting or were surprised, Allectus was defeated.

In the light of these historical events in the second half of the 3rd century AD it is easy to imagine the two magistrates and the members of the *curia* of the *civitas* of the Regni wanting to protect their chief town. Perhaps they were encouraged in this by higher authority, given forceful backing and even subsidised to some extent. Approval would still have been needed from an imperial authority, but we may imagine that this would have been more readily forthcoming from a pretender to that authority, such as the Gallic empire, or later the British-based empire of Carausius and, after him, Allectus. Receiving, possibly inviting an application for fortification and then bestowing approval would have substantiated the pretender's claim to authority, apart from the military utility of a fortified town near the south coast. The walls were indeed a substantial defence, capable of being manned to keep out attackers and besiegers. In this respect Noviomagus, as a fortified town, may have been considered a link in the chain of fortified places on which the naval and land forces of the Saxon shore were based. Durovernum, although a town, may

have been fortified at least in part for the same reason. There is some uncertainty as to how these fortified bases operated and what function they really served. Perhaps their military functions changed as time went by, and in any case those fortified centres that were also towns presumably continued to operate as far as possible as civil settlements and markets, too. How different would life be in a fortified town? Who operated these defences, if not soldiers? The simplest use of them would have been to control who and what entered and left a town. Only a few relatively untrained personnel would have been needed to watch the gates, and perhaps close them during the hours of darkness. Such a force could probably have been recruited and paid by the same *ordo* that built the walls in the first place.

By the 3rd century AD there was a sense, in contrast to the situation before, that towns should possess walls for prestige as well as security. It was how substantial towns identified themselves and were recognised. Even if walls were regarded as a kind of civic status symbol, however, they were not a sham. Their utility as a symbol would depend ultimately on their capability of being used as a real defence. At a minimum this has the archaeological implication that walls were continuous linear features, without unfilled gaps, and they would be functional, however much they may also have been for show. Their visible strength would have had a deterrent value, too. Town walls had become a potent sign of civilisation.

18 Roman 'gladius' used by legionary soldiers (the blade is 520mm long) – a surviving iron blade and a modern reconstruction

19 Late Roman coins from Chichester – from left: debased silver antoninianus; silver denarius of Septimius Severus; coin of Caracalla incorporated into a late 3rd-/early 4th-century AD silver signet ring

4

Defending the Roman town: bastions and towers

ADDING BASTIONS OR TOWERS TO THE WALLS

At some later time, probably in the 4th century AD, the existing walls of Noviomagus were reinforced by the addition of a number of bastions or towers to the outer face of the masonry wall. The remains or traces of eight can still be seen, all but one in the southern half of the circuit of the walls, and others have been excavated. The most obvious remains of these bastions are where the upstanding wall has been least disturbed by subsequent development, along the south side of the garden of the Bishop's Palace and the Deanery, for instance, and to the south-east of the former Cawley Priory (now the District Council's offices and a public car park). This latter zone outside the upstanding wall was where the course of the River Lavant was diverted at some later time, which probably explains its relative neglect and underdevelopment. The biggest of the remaining bastions are still markedly reduced and smaller in size than they were originally, having been eroded and robbed of their constituent materials in the same way as the masonry wall has been (Chapter 5).

All the bastions that have been investigated appear to have been very like each other, implying that they were all built to a single design and probably added, therefore, in a single programme of work. The typical bastion, in plan, was about 5m wide and projected forward from the outer face of the upstanding wall for a distance of about 5m with, projecting further forward, a simple semicircular face about 2.5m in radius. This shape was probably chosen, at least in part, because the bastions were to be solid and built in fairly amorphous materials that could not be laid to uniform

1 Part of the wall on the south side of the Bishop's Palace garden, with the Palace bastion

courses and form well-finished corners, unlike ashlar masonry. The original plan can be recovered from the foundations of the bastions, which were massive and carefully prepared, presumably because of the solidity and height of their superstructure. The typical bastion projected as far as the existing ditch, the inner lip of which may have been as little as 5m from the wall; the nearer side of the ditch, therefore, had to be reinforced under the front of the bastions. It used to be thought this ditch was completely filled in, at least where the bastions were to be placed, but excavations in the south-west quadrant in 2010 have shown that this was not the case. The front edge of the foundations for the bastions was built more strongly than the sides, and made rectangular in plan. The latter shape would have had the benefit of spreading the load of the superstructure to either side rather than directly forward into the ditch, and may have been easier to construct using large, rectangular blocks of stone. Several of the stones in the lower part of the foundations were reused, the fact of their former use elsewhere being indicated by the presence on them of redundant mouldings, traces of earlier mortar and signs of weathering on what, later, were hidden faces. The front edge of the foundations was stepped down, to spread the load better and securely anchor the front of the bastion in the side of the ditch. The base of the external face of the bastion was marked by a plinth course of stone with a chamfered upper corner. The foundations and footings along the straight stretch on either side of the bastion were extended further outwards by a short distance. This is most unlikely to have been the base of an offset or kink continuing upwards on the external face of the superstructure where the semicircular face met the straight faces, which would have necessitated some complicated quoining using much better dressed stone than has been seen in the core or the foundations and would have been vulnerable to damage. Instead, this offset probably existed only at foundation level, where it was intended to spread the load of the superstructure more securely to either side and provide a suitable footing for the rest of the bastion.

The outer half of the bastion foundations consisted of blocks of chalk laid in white mortar, whereas the inner half was simply rammed chalk, tipped into the foundation trench and tamped down. This trench stopped short of the face of the existing upstanding wall, leaving a gap up to 0.3m wide where the bastion would not have been deeply founded. Presumably, although the bastion foundation trenches were not necessarily dug very deeply, this gap was left so as not to undermine the existing wall.

At the front of the bastion the gaps in the outer corners of the foundations, between the large blocks of stone forming the edges of the rectangular foundations and the semicircular footings of the

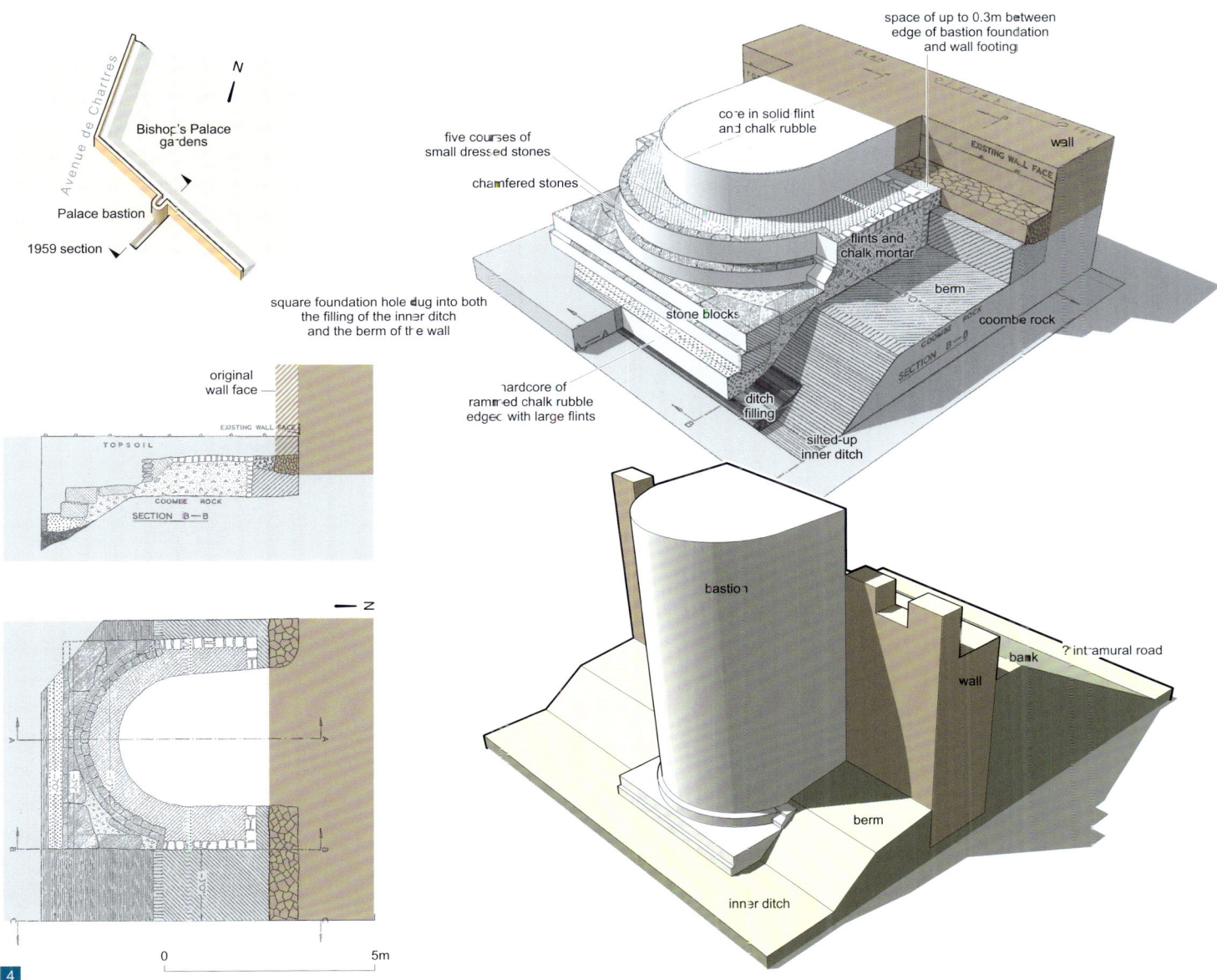

space of up to 0.3m between
edge of bastion foundation
and wall footing

core in solid flint
and chalk rubble

five courses of
small dressed stones

chamfered stones

wall

EXISTING WALL FACE

flints and
chalk mortar

berm

stone blocks

coombe rock

SECTION B—B

square foundation hole dug into both
the filling of the inner ditch
and the berm of the wall

hardcore of
rammed chalk rubble
edged with large flints

ditch
filling

silted-up
inner ditch

original
wall face

EXISTING WALL FACE

TOPSOIL

COOMBE ROCK

SECTION B—B

Avenue de Chartres

N

Bishop's Palace
gardens

Palace bastion

1959 section

bastion

? intramural road

bank

wall

berm

inner ditch

0   5m

4

superstructure, were filled with flints in mortar. Elsewhere small dressed stones were laid in hard pink mortar to form a base for the superstructure. The core of the superstructure, which survives in places, comprised nodules and large fragments of flint, lumps of chalk and clunch, and occasional fragments of various other stones laid randomly in yellow or white sandy lime mortar. This mixture of materials is in contrast with the fairly uniform character of the core of the linear wall. The presence of 'a piece of pink mortar and a worked ashlar stone' within the core of a bastion newly exposed in an early archaeological excavation was taken by Ian Hannah in 1934, correctly, as evidence of the reuse of materials from other buildings. The further conclusion that the bastion was constructed in haste does not necessarily follow, however.

The core would have been unsuitable to be left exposed as a face, and a similar method of constructing the face seems to have been employed as that used in the linear wall, in successive lifts or builds. The outer face was probably built first, a short lift at a time, and the core added, lift by lift. Repairs in 2011 to the Residentiary bastion in the south-west quadrant have revealed a small patch of the original face surviving at a surprisingly high level, nearly 4m above ground level. This consists of roughly squared flints laid with flush

---

2 The bastion at Market Avenue during excavations in 1956

3 Details of the Market Avenue bastion footings, from above

4 Reconstruction of the Palace bastion based on the excavation records shown

faces outwards, set in the same mid yellow, sandy lime mortar as the core behind them. By contrast, for a height of roughly 1.5m from the base of the superstructure the mortar used in the facing was pozzolanic; that is, it contains finely ground ceramic that makes it more resistant to moisture and weathering, like hydraulic cement, and gives it a distinctly pink colour. The facing stones themselves do not survive there, but the pink mortar could be seen behind the facing, running in thin bands into the core, each band presumably indicating where the construction of individual lifts of the facing had resumed after the core had been built up to that level.

Interestingly, the superstructure of the bastions seems not to have been bonded securely with the outer face of the upstanding masonry wall. Where this junction has been excavated, the superstructure core was simply butted to the existing wall face, and mortared. The face of the earlier wall was thus preserved in these patches relatively undisturbed, although the character of these patches is not always the same and some of them, at least, may therefore be repairs (Chapter 3).

In addition to reinforcement wherever necessary the existing ditch or ditches may have been recut. These may already have become partially blocked anyway as a result of the weathering of the upper slopes of their sides and the accumulation of flood deposits and debris. One or more new ditches may have been dug a short distance further away from the existing wall and the projecting bastions or, possibly, any existing outer ditch was simply redug. A series of ditches excavated in 2005 in the north-east quadrant suggests that different actions may have been undertaken in different places. It seems unlikely that anyone would have gone to the trouble of deliberately infilling either of the existing ditches unless this were clearly necessary; they are more likely to have wanted to redig such ditches or augment them with new ditches. Broken ground in front of a defensive wall and bastions was not in itself objectionable so long as it gave attackers no advantage. Where would the very large quantity of material upcast from newly excavated, and possibly broader, ditches have gone? Two answers can be offered. Firstly, some of the material may have been washed away by the River Lavant in flood. Secondly, the

upcast could have been used as road metalling or, within the town, to infill wet hollows and level up the ground as necessary. The material was not used in the core of the bastions, as it would have been unsuitable.

DISCUSSION

This discussion considers the purpose, and therefore the form, of these additions to the defences of Noviomagus, their date and what their construction may tell us about the town at that time. The character of the bastions from the level of the wall walk upwards, assuming they rose higher, depends on their purpose and this, it has frequently been said, was to act as platforms for the mechanical artillery of the time. There seems to be no definite archaeological or documentary evidence to support this interpretation, however. Contemporary mechanical artillery, such as catapults and counter-weighted swing-firing devices, seem to have been used at fairly long range, and commonly as siege weapons to break walls down. If they were to be used as long-range defensive weapons from a raised wall it would seem to have been easier and safer to have built platforms for them just inside the line of the wall. At Noviomagus, for instance, they could have been placed on platforms of earth added to, or even dug into, the existing bank on the inner face of the wall. The range of these weapons would be increased if they were given extra height, but for this purpose there is no evidence to suggest that they could not have been put on timber structures, which presumably would have stood up to any recoil and wear and tear as well as the timber frame of the weapons themselves would do. Indeed, by the same reasoning, if these weapons were to be put on a masonry structure at all it does not follow that this structure would have had to be solid masonry. A hollow bastion with a timber floor would have served equally well, and many examples of hollow masonry bastions or towers are known, the most relevant being those at the nearest Saxon shore forts at Portchester and Pevensey, among others. These were built integrally with the surrounding wall, but they project from the outer face of the wall, with semicircular outer ends, just as the bastions or towers did at Noviomagus. Smaller mechanical devices such as crossbows (ballistae) could well have been mounted on bastions and towers, but they do not seem to explain the large size and form of the structures that were built. The main advantage offered by a tower or bastion projecting from the outer face of a wall is that the projection allows the defenders to fire their weapons (spears, slingshots and arrows) along the length of the wall to either side. Mechanical artillery would seem not to be suitable for such flanking fire at relatively close range, especially if adjacent bastions were close together. To build the bastions for this purpose alone would seem to have been extravagant and unnecessary. They could have been used as artillery platforms, but this was not necessarily their primary purpose.

The solidity of the bastions suggests that they were built to carry considerable superstructure, more than simply their own mass up to the level of the wall walk, although solidity was also a defence against demolition by a besieger's artillery, battering rams and sappers. The superstructure would presumably have been hollow from the level of the wall walk upwards, to enable defenders to get to loopholes in the face of the structure. The length of the projecting sides, indeed, would probably have accommodated more than one loophole. We do not know how high the structures originally rose, but it would seem reasonable to suppose that they contained at least one floor internally at the level of the

5 Bastion being added to the wall (Fred van Deelen)

6 Items of Roman military armour and weaponry – from left: bronze strap end; cuirass hinge plate; two lorica hinges; bronze crest knob from legionary helmet; bronze helmet carrying handle

wall walk and at least one more floor above. An important reason for additional height would have been to give defenders a good view out; tall towers are useful lookouts and vital in a siege. Furthermore, the bastions could have been roofed whereas the wall walk was probably open to the sky. The structures, therefore, are to be interpreted as impressive, projecting interval towers, although the term 'bastion' is now sanctioned by long archaeological use.

The intervals at which the bastion towers were built is not known for certain, and need not have been exactly regular. Excavations in 2010 in front of the wall in the south-west quarter have demonstrated that a bastion tower existed there at a distance of about 30m from its neighbours to either side. Elsewhere in the circuit there seem to have been bastion towers at intervals of, variously, 30m, 44m and 77m. At least six bastions are known in the northern half of the circuit, either directly from their remains or on the strength of reasonable documentary evidence, while at least 11 are known in the southern half. Negative evidence, that is, excavations in front of the wall that have found definitely that no bastion was built there, must also be taken into account. Different possible schemes can be suggested, including the known bastions and additional bastion towers conjectured at different intervals, but they remain to be confirmed by excavation or non-intrusive geophysical survey. The most useful conclusion to be drawn at the moment is that the bastion towers seem to have been surprisingly closely spaced on the southern side of the circuit, and were possibly less closely spaced on the northern side.

The bastions or towers seem to have been added in a single phase of work, although how long this lasted is uncertain. The volume of a single bastion, from ground level up to the level of the existing wall walk, would have been about 140m³ and the material for this, using the assumptions in earlier calculations for the work entailed in constructing the masonry wall (Chapter 3), would have weighed some 210 metric tons. The upper superstructure, if forming another stage in each tower, would probably account for some 37m³ of stone and mortar weighing 56 tonnes, for a total in each bastion tower of 266 tonnes. The 11 known bastion towers would therefore total 2926 tonnes, and the possibility of perhaps ten more would give an overall total of 5586 tonnes. Calculating how long it would take to transport this material to the construction site on the same basis as used above for the first phase of the walls (200 pack animals and 40 draught animals for 150 days per year) gives an answer of about six years. They could probably have been built even more quickly if circumstances required.

The exact date of the addition of the bastion towers is not known, but it is clear that they are characteristic of late Roman fortifications. Externally projecting towers of this type were common from the 3rd century AD onwards, whereas earlier towers on a wall had been internally projecting. As well as having practical purposes, towers were meant to impress, intimidate and deter any would-be attacker. Moreover, adding towers to the existing wall at Noviomagus may have been a matter of military-civic fashion, in keeping with a perception that fortified towns or, rather, fortified places of any kind were somehow incomplete without the new style towers. Perhaps the original plan, which would otherwise deserve to be called old-fashioned and a little plain, had included towers such as these and the plan had to wait for enough resources to be available to be completed as intended.

The political and military situation in Britain started reasonably well in the 4th century AD. After Constantius died at York his son, Constantine, was acclaimed there as emperor by Constantius's army. Constantine turned out to be an able, lucky and long-lived ruler. Huge changes occurred in his reign, such as the adoption of Christianity as the state religion and the elevation of the emperor to appear as a remote, semi-divine figure at the centre of a hierarchical, ritual-bound court. A different kind of machinery of state came into existence as did, parallel to this, the apparatus of the Christian Church. The army liked dynastic continuity. Emperors wanted religious uniformity. The emperor, now nominally

7

8

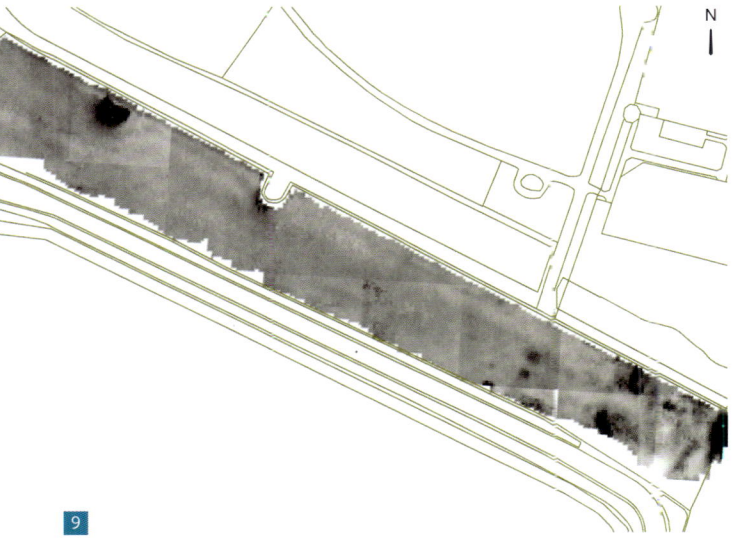

in Constantine's new Rome of Constantinople (Istanbu , Turkey), delegated power to regional leaders, such as the Prefect of the Gauls, responsible for what were called the dioceses of Britain and Spain as well as Gaul. Dioceses were subdivided into provinces, smaller than before. The control and organisation of the army was by this time separate from the distribution and management of provinces, and it was under the command of generals who bore new titles such as *dux* and *comes* (from which, much ater, 'duke' and 'count' were derived); the commander of the Saxon shore, for instance, was a *comes*. Men of barbarian ancestry made the late Roman army their life, and Constantine, who admired Germanic peoples, created military units drawn from such peoples living both inside and outside the empire. Zosimus, writing some time after these events, noted that Constantine transferred soldiers from frontier camps to towns, which were duly fortified as a result. The military reason for this may have been to ensure that Roman territory was defended in depth, as well as at its boundaries, against incursions from outside, incursions which had become a continual threat.

A hugely increased and militarised bureaucracy was responsible for supplying the army, for which purpose it raised taxes and obtained goods and materials in kind. For instance, a state-run factory in Britain making woollen clothing for the army is documented in the 4th century AD at 'Venta', quite likely to be Winchester; one of three towns in Britain with this name. If so, the wool probably came from sheep grazing on the Downs, and Noviomagus would have been an obvious place for collecting the wool and selling it on to Venta. The first half of the 4th century AD seems to have been a time of great prosperity in Britain, at least for the owners of great villas in the countryside, attested by the expansion and decoration of their buildings, which in turn presumably reflects the profitability of their surrounding estates. Many villas and, therefore, country estates existed within a short distance of Noviomagus, on the coastal plain and in the foothills of the Downs and beyond, and their owners were probably among the *curiales* largely responsible for paying for construction of the walls of Noviomagus.

7   The bastions provided a good look-out and base for counter-attack for defenders of the town (Fred van Deelen)

8   Bronze coin of Constantine

9   The results of a geophysical survey of the land outside the south wall of the Bishop's Palace garden reveal the location of one of the 'missing' bastions as a dark spot, west of the Palace bastion

10   Excavations to uncover and record the newly located bastion in 2010

The economy of towns was probably also directed increasingly to providing for the army and the bureaucracy. A fortified town was partly a military base, in itself, and in the 4th century AD towns are documented as having to maintain soldiers who were billeted to them. The town defences would have to be manned in time of need, and the townspeople themselves, relatively untrained and inexperienced, would probably have been able to accomplish only a small amount on their own.

Why would the existing defences of Noviomagus have been reinforced, if this were not simply the completion of the original design? From the middle years of the 4th century AD onwards the political and military situation in Britain, as elsewhere in the Roman world, dramatically worsened. Imperial forces had to retake control of Britain, by force or subterfuge, on three occasions in the mid to late 4th century AD, as had happened once in the 3rd century AD, and the politics of this were complicated by a doctrinal dimension. People were divided between Christians and adherents of other religions, and Christians were divided doctrinally among themselves. The reimposition of imperial authority was accompanied by religious bigotry and purges. Different authorities may have promulgated a policy of refortifying towns on these occasions (in AD 343 and 360), to give protection to (or from) the armed forces of different sides. Protection against seaborne raiders from outside the empire, and from pirates, may have been

a reason for instituting defences around Noviomagus in the 3rd century AD, but was probably not in itself a reason for later augmenting these defences. Concerted raids across the frontier in Britain and attacks on Gaul are famously documented in AD 367, possibly including treachery by Germanic mercenaries and the surrender of at least one of Britain's provinces. The consequent anarchy and ruin may have been exaggerated by later writers, but even this could accurately reflect contemporary perceptions, from which would have flowed decisions to reinforce towns as well as the willingness to pay for such protection. Unfortunately the tax burden was increasing just when the tax base was diminishing; the number of *curiales* must have been depleted, while at the same time exemption from taxes and contributory obligations was extended to churchmen, bureaucratic office-holders and the military.

More may have been done at this time to protect Noviomagus than adding bastion towers to the wall and, at least in places, recutting and enlarging the ditches. Circumstantial evidence suggests that the south gate may have been blocked. Certainly the fact that the eventual later redevelopment of the streets of the town excluded the former south gate, medieval South Street leading to a different crossing of the line of the walls a short distance to the west, implies that the original south gate was not functioning then (Chapter 5). Perhaps the south gate had been damaged in some way and was regarded as beyond repair. If the south gate were

11

blocked deliberately this would imply that keeping the direct route open to the nearest landing place in Chichester harbour was less important than protecting the town from possible attack from this direction.

Britain was less damaged by conflict in the 4th century AD than Gaul, and the attempts mounted from the Continent to regain control of its resources were made so strenuously partly for this reason, as Britain was still a net contributor in goods and materials to the army elsewhere. Eventually, however, imperial forces on the Continent were no longer able by the beginning of the 5th century AD even to attempt to retake Britain, and the former strong interconnection with the rest of the Roman world seems rather suddenly and effectively to have lapsed. What little we know of the town points to its almost complete depopulation at the end of the 4th and beginning of the 5th centuries AD. Although we have no definite evidence for what may have happened in and around Noviomagus at this time, it is possible that in the course of events the town's defences were damaged or slighted.

---

11 The site of the Deanery bastion, with a small section of the face of the original linear wall surviving where the bastion had been built in front of it

12 Late Roman Chichester, mid to late 4th century AD

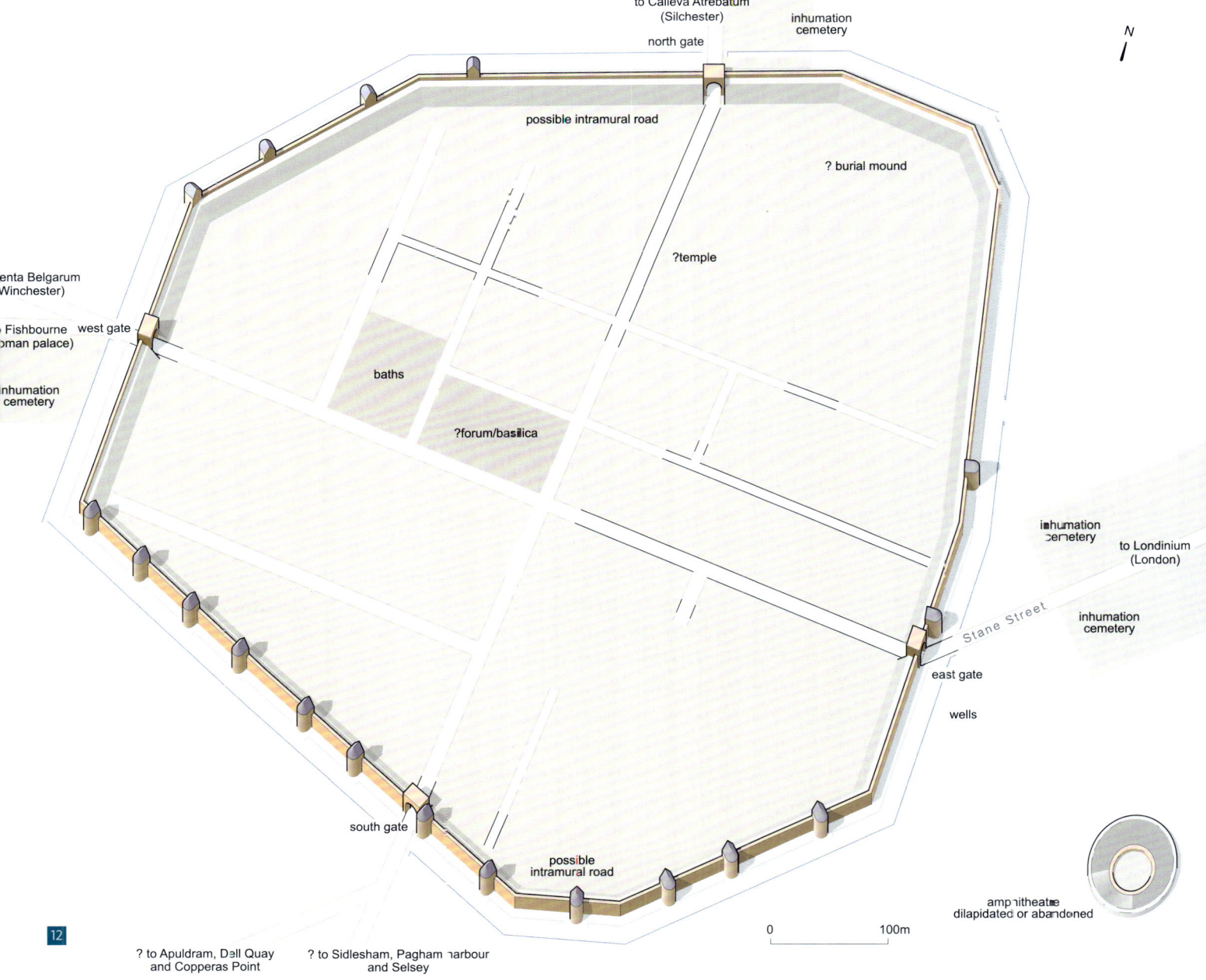

to Calleva Atrebatum (Silchester)

inhumation cemetery

north gate

N

possible intramural road

? burial mound

?temple

Venta Belgarum (Winchester)

Fishbourne (Roman palace)   west gate

inhumation cemetery

baths

?forum/basilica

inhumation cemetery

to Londinium (London)

Stane Street

inhumation cemetery

east gate

wells

south gate

possible intramural road

amphitheatre dilapidated or abandoned

12

? to Apuldram, Dell Quay and Copperas Point

? to Sidlesham, Pagham harbour and Selsey

0   100m

5

An Anglo-Saxon kingdom and shire

The entry of Germanic peoples into Britain, which had begun little by little in the 4th century AD, resulted eventually in the establishment from the 5th century AD onwards of several regional chiefdoms, in time dignified by the name of kingdoms. Sussex, the kingdom of the South Saxons, was not the largest, richest or most advanced of these. The archaeological evidence of cemeteries if not occupation, indicates that Anglo-Saxon settlement spread slowly from east to west in Sussex and the site of the Roman town of Chichester, at the western end of this advance, seems to have been practically deserted for a period of nearly 500 years, until quite late in the history of Anglo-Saxon Sussex. Whether it was the walls that deterred settlement is unclear, but otherwise they seem to have had little significance at first. The interior of the former Roman town would not necessarily have been attractive to settlement: ruinous, its buildings would have been roofless, crumbling and overgrown, and its streets impassably choked with vegetation. In abandoned towns the development to a depth of as much as 1m of a soil rich in humus and charcoal, dark earth, has been attributed to the unchecked growth over a period of many years of lime-loving vegetation in fairly sheltered conditions, both rooting downwards and reworking the uppermost deposits of the former settlement and accumulating upwards. Left to themselves, Chichester's defensive walls, too, would have been subject to severe dilapidation caused by rooting of vegetation, water ingress, frosting and then collapse. If the walls had already been slighted or damaged, as could have happened in the late 4th or early 5th centuries AD, these processes would have started at once. Some of the outer facing stones of both the masonry wall and the bastion towers would have fallen off, taking the crenellated parapets with them. The constituent stones of both the face and the core were probably sufficiently squared and closely fitting to be able to resist subsequent natural erosion, especially in the absence of extensive periodic courses of tiles which, elsewhere seem to some degree to have protected the stones beneath them. The mortar in the core would have disintegrated and washed out from between the flints, which would then have become loosened and liable to be dislodged. The consequence of several centuries of unchecked decay and dilapidation may have been the weathering and infilling of the ditches, the collapse of the bastion towers and the exposure of the core of the masonry wall and its progressive erosion back by perhaps as much as half its bulk, at least in its upper more exposed part. The debris could have tumbled and piled up at the base of the exposed and eroding core, forming a kind of talus of bare flint nodules. Without new inhabitants in the town, or much need for flint round about, this scene may have been long undisturbed.

The inhabitants of the region, whether surviving Romano-Britons or incoming Anglo-Saxons, probably lived close to a subsistence level, mainly by farming, coastal fishing and seafaring. By the late 7th century AD at least two places near Chichester are thought to have been of equal or greater significance than the former Noviomagus, namely Bosham, to the west, and Selsey, to the south. Bosham, which significantly takes its name probably from an early Anglo-Saxon settler, was part of an extensive estate on the coast stretching into Hampshire. The eastern half of this estate, including the village and harbour of Bosham, eventually came into the possession of Earl Godwinson, for whom it was a rudimentary kind of naval base. Selsey, by contrast, has a topographically derived name from 'seal island', according to Bede's 8th-century AD *Ecclesiastical History of the English People*. Nevertheless, it had some inhabitants, the focus of whose settlement was probably Pagham harbour. Modern reclamation masks the estuarine marshes that, by Bede's time early in the 8th century AD, were a most cutting Selsey off from the mainland. Bede notes all this because his Northumbrian colleague, Wilfrid, had chosen this spot to build a minster. Some years before this foundation, Wilfrid had been shipwrecked on Selsey and considered himself lucky to escape with his life from the pagan inhabitants. He returned in due course to evangelise among the South Saxons, who were among the last Anglo-Saxons to convert to Christianity and, with the support of their king, he began in c AD 680 to construct the buildings that would constitute a minster, probably at Church Norton (Sussex) on the south side of Pagham harbour (also known as Wythering). It must be significant that Wilfrid's minster was not inside the former Roman town of Noviomagus and the royal backing took the form of a gift of land, the produce of which would support the minster community. From the 8th century AD onwards, more seaborne raiders from the Continent, variously called Norsemen, Vikings and Danes, began to attack settlements along the east and south coasts of Britain. The South Saxon kingdom was unable to defend itself and, partly for that reason, fell under the sway in the AD 770s of Mercia, centred on the Midlands, and then in AD 825, of Wessex, centred on the south-west of England.

Chichester is first documented by that name in the Anglo-Saxon Chronicle, spelled *cisseceastre* and, later, *cycester*. Contemporary coins Latinise the name as *cissa civ[itas]*. The fact that no element of its original Romano-British name survived may indicate a complete discontinuity of occupation in, and local knowledge of, the town, unlike the case, for instance, of the first element in Winchester, which clearly derives from Venta. The Chronicle contains a kind of foundation story, explaining the first element of the new name Chichester by saying it was derived from the name of a supposed pioneer Anglo-Saxon settler, Cissa, one of three sons of Aelle, whom the Chronicle says landed in Sussex in the 5th century AD. The names of other pioneers recorded in this way seem to have been derived by a combination of learned and folk etymology from later place names simply to try and explain the origin of the latter. These explanatory derivations are not to be taken at face value. An alternative derivation of the first element of 'Chichester' may conceivably be from the Old English word for gravel, shingle and pebbles, from which other place names such as Chislehurst (Kent) and Chesil Beach (Dorset) are derived. The second element is an unexceptional Anglicisation of the Latin *castrum* or *castra*, meaning a fortification, commonly used in the Anglo-Saxon names of former Romano-British walled towns, such as Winchester. If the derivation of the first element of the name Chichester is correct it may refer, not to the character of the local natural topography, although that would be reasonable to expect, but actually to the character of the fortifications. The complete name would then be a descriptive toponym, meaning something like 'pebbly fortification', perhaps from the appearance of the ruined walls.

The next mention of Chichester is rather more reliable. The late 9th- and early 10th-century AD Burghal Hidage records some of the practical arrangements for defending a number of places in southern England, organised by Alfred, king of Wessex, and his successors in an extensive programme of resistance to the Danes. Chichester was one such burh, a fortified base that could if necessary shelter an army and, equally importantly, be readily defended so as to deny its possible shelter to an enemy. Many of the 30 burhs named were former towns in Roman Britain with walls, like Chichester, and in those cases the existence of such walls was doubtless what led to their being chosen. The fortification, or refortification, of these burhs was put in hand probably from the late AD 870s onwards. The inhabitants of the country round about each burh were given the tasks of constructing, maintaining and garrisoning the burh; every hide of land assigned to a burh was to supply one man for all these tasks, and every pole of the burh's defences was to be held by four men in time of need, perhaps operating in rotation or with some of them acting as a reserve. Putting aside for the moment the actual area of a hide of land, the relation between the numbers of a garrison and the length of the defences, measured in poles, is highly informative. A pole is equivalent to five and a half yards or 16 feet 6 inches (5.0m). The length of the walls of Chichester, including the gates, at the present day is some 2377m and, as this length seems not to have changed in the interim, we may suppose that it was probably measured in the 9th century AD as being 472 poles. The number of hides allocated to Chichester was 1500 which, though it looks suspiciously like a rounded number, is not likely to be, judging by the precision of other entries and the practical purpose of the document, and thus may be taken as the number of men required for Chichester's defence. At the ratio of four men to every pole, we would expect the defences to have measured 375 poles (about 1886m). What can account for the apparent discrepancy of 97 poles (about 488m)?

It has been shown that discrepancies of this kind in the calculated lengths of the defences at other burhs in the Burghal Hidage, such as Portchester, Southampton (Hampshire) and Lyng (Somerset), can be accounted for by a portion of the defences being protected

1

2

by water or marsh, which therefore did not need to be actively manned. At Chichester, too, part of the circuit of the walls on the south could have been protected by the River Lavant and marshy ground. The River Lavant used to flow directly from north to south at some distance to the east of the Roman town (Chapter 2), but at some later time its course changed so that it flowed from east to west around the southern part of the city walls (as it still does). How far to the west did it flow and at which times? Documentary evidence exists for the river taking different courses in medieval and early post-medieval times depending on its flow and strength, and the earliest maps to usefully show the Lavant's course (from 1610 onwards) vary in what they show. If the 9th-century AD measurements are correct, they would suggest that at that time, when Chichester's defences were revived, slightly more length of wall had to be defended than may seem to have been required on the basis of much later observation of the Lavant.

The implied 9th- and 10th-century AD documentary evidence for the later westward course of the Lavant gives us a *terminus ante quem*, a date before which the river must have begun to take a new course. The diversion of the river need not have been achieved solely by human agency. The existence of the ditches around the walls, and the probability of flooding in conditions of more rudimentary agriculture and rising sea level, suggest that this diversion may have occurred naturally in time of flood and afterwards been artificially made permanent. It seems likely that the new course was encouraged in order to make defending the city easier, even though only a quarter or so of the circuit of the walls would have been thus protected by the river; the defenders would have welcomed not having to guard so much of the walls, provided that the unmanned sector was safely fronted by river and marsh. Of more everyday use, the diverted river could have powered a water mill. Domesday Book records a mill somewhere at Chichester by 1066, and a mill situated probably just outside

the east gate is documented in the 14th century, although by then there were at least two other mills, the King's Water Mill or Lavant Mill on Stane Street some 200m to the east of the east gate and another outside the west gate.

How were the walls of the burh made defensible at the end of the 9th century AD, especially if the masonry wall and the bastion towers had by then become badly dilapidated and were without a crenellated parapet? The first task was probably to clear the debris from the base of the masonry wall and bastion towers. The eroded flint nodules and, at the lowest level, the fallen facing stones and coping stones would have been removed both to make a more effective barrier of the remaining masonry and to reuse as building material. At least one ditch would presumably have been redug, although by then the whole area outside the south-east quadrant of the walls was probably impassably marshy and seasonally flooded, and the ditches were therefore not necessarily continuous. The defenders of the burh will have wanted to make the top of the masonry wall both accessible to themselves and easily defensible in some way, perhaps by adding timbers to form a palisaded walkway; although, as the top of the wall and bank have not survived, there is no firm evidence for how the defences were restored. The systematic refacing of the outer face of the masonry wall, where it is likely that the core of the wall was not only completely exposed but also cut back quite raggedly, would have been a much greater undertaking for which the defenders may not

---

1 A pair of gilded cast bronze saucer brooches from the Anglo-Saxon cemetery at Apple Down

2 Anglo-Saxon burhs, minsters and ports in and near the western half of Sussex

3 Late 5th-/early 6th-century AD items from the cemetery at Apple Down – from left: gilded cast bronze brooch; gilded small square-headed brooch; gilded cast copper-alloy belt buckle and plate with garnets

have been equipped. Perhaps they limited themselves to filling in the larger holes and irregularities, so that the exposed core could not easily be climbed. We do not know the extent to which the bastion towers had been reduced in height, although it is assumed that the outer face of these, too, had largely or wholly gone. The existing gates were likely to have been less damaged than the wall, in so far as they were probably constructed of larger, squared stone blocks, less susceptible to wholesale disintegration by weathering. The west, north and east gates may still have been passable, but if the ground had built up around them their headroom may have been commensurately lower. The south gate may have been impassable (as mentioned in Chapter 4; see also below).

The defenders of the burh, who were presumably also the rebuilders of its walls, would have come from hamlets and farmsteads in the countryside around Chichester. The number of men required, 1500, was a levy; they would have manned the defences in rotation, and some of them could have formed a reserve. A hide of land was nominally 120 acres (48.5ha), so the area required to provide this number of men at the rate of one hide per man would amount to 180,000 acres or 281 square miles (72,800ha or 72km^2); it can be visualised as an area roughly 8–9km square on the coastal plain. That the defenders were active is clear from a reference in the Anglo-Saxon Chronicle for the year AD 895, when a Danish raiding force on its way back

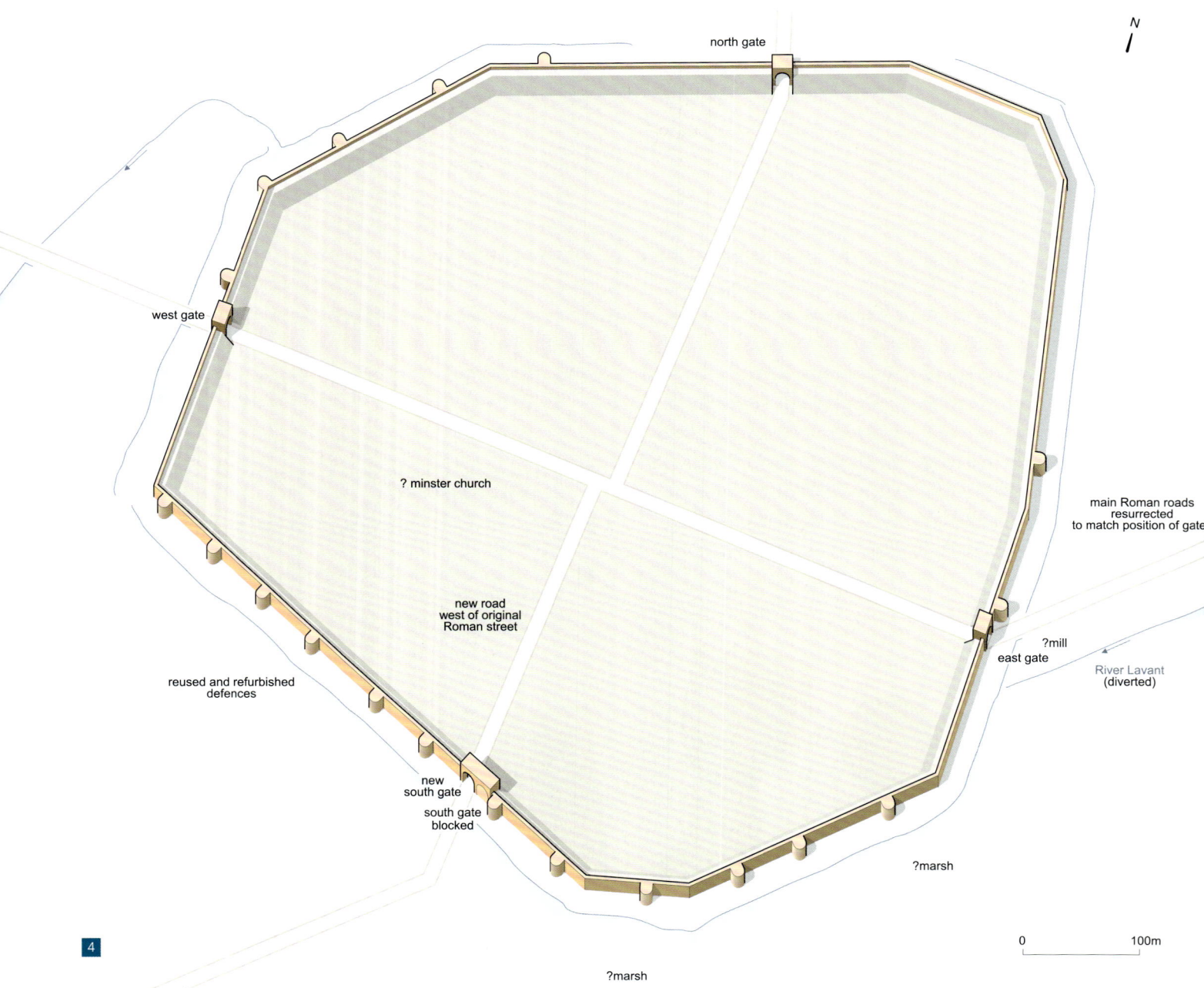

north gate

N

west gate

? minster church

main Roman roads
resurrected
to match position of gate

new road
west of original
Roman street

?mill

east gate

River Lavant
(diverted)

reused and refurbished
defences

new
south gate

south gate
blocked

?marsh

4

0   100m

?marsh

home from plundering Exeter put in close to Chichester where, perhaps unexpectedly, 'the townsmen slew many hundreds of them and put them to flight and burned some of their ships'. The term translated as 'townsmen' could mean burh-defenders and need not mean inhabitants of the town. We have no evidence that more than a very few people would have been living within the walls; only one or two possible dwellings have been excavated, near the east gate for instance.

By the 10th century AD Chichester is documented as having, like other burhs, at least one moneyer who minted coins, taking the necessary dies from London, as did all the other moneyers of Wessex and, later in the 10th century AD, of the English kingdom. This implies, although the evidence is not definite, that Chichester had become a port, a term then applied inland as well as on the coast meaning a market place regulated by the king, where dues and tolls could be efficiently collected and transactions properly witnessed, and therefore made enforceable. The further implication is that the town within the walls had been opened to passage and settlement. This was a formative time in the history of the city, in which the remains of the walls played an important part.

In reviving the town, two or three main streets were laid out, perhaps starting with the street running from east to west. When the first medieval streets were formed in former Romano-British towns it seems that their direction and alignment could sometimes be determined by simple desire-lines aiming to and coming from the surviving gates or perhaps newly made openings in the surrounding walls, and perhaps by a need to avoid obstacles. It was unlikely that there would have been anything directly visible of the actual former streets themselves. In Chichester's case the main east–west street could have been formed by people going in roughly a straight line between the east and west gates, or what remained of them. The streets to and from the north and south gates do not fit this pattern, however. North Street was laid out roughly at right angles to the east–west street, running straight to the existing north gate. In the opposite direction the former south gate (Chapter 3) was apparently impassable and no effort was made to open and reuse it; perhaps too much masonry had collapsed. Instead, another opening was made through the south-west quadrant of the walls only 10–15m to the west of the former gate (implying that this was beyond the original gatehouse), and South Street was laid out running straight through the new gate. Very significantly, South Street was also laid out at right angles to the east–west street, and moreover was

continued in a straight line for almost the same distance beyond the walls as within them.

If North Street and South Street had been based on desire-lines alone, we might have expected them to form a single street in a straight line between the north gate and the new south gate, or some other set of lines altogether. The actual rectilinear layout strongly suggests that the two main streets running to the north and south gates were meant to serve as the basis for a fairly regular grid of plots of land aligned to them and to the main east–west street. The earliest accurate map of Chichester, by Gardner in 1769, clearly shows narrow burgage plots running away at right angles from these streets and from other side streets parallel to them, such as St Martin's Lane and Little London, to the east of North Street, and the Upper West Lanes (now Chapel Street), to the west, and North Pallant and South Pallant to the east of South Street. Plainly the main streets were laid out first, anticipating the regular subdivision of the land between them, and it would be reasonable to suppose that this was done when the burh was instituted. Certainly this would have had to coincide with the creation of the new south gate in the walls.

A Late Saxon minster is also documented in the town, thought to have been the forerunner of the parish church of St Peter the Great, which was incorporated in the later cathedral. It may be that the original minster church was situated somewhere to the south of West Street, where the grid apparently did not extend. The hard metalling of Roman streets, if it could be detected, was often used for a foundation for subsequent buildings, especially if the latter were large.

If as much as a third of the volume of the masonry wall around Chichester had become dislodged and in being cleared away had to be reused, to what uses were all this valuable building stone put? While most dwellings and similar buildings inside the walls and outside would have been of timber and clay, the nodules of flint and the blocks or fragments of dressed stone would probably have gone, firstly to patching and repairing the masonry defences themselves, secondly towards building the minster in Chichester and churches both there and elsewhere, and lastly for other purposes for which the stone may have been best suited, such as surfacing the new streets or for ballast in seagoing boats.

4　Anglo-Saxon Chichester, 8th to 9th centuries AD

6

A Norman castle, county and diocese

When the king of England, the chaste and saintly Edward the Confessor, died childless in January 1066, the country must have appeared an attractive prize. The throne was taken by the nearest claimant, Harold Godwinson, Earl of Wessex, probably the richest and most powerful person in the country and already its de facto ruler, who said that Edward had named him as his successor. The Godwin family's wealth was based on their landholdings in Sussex, including control of Chichester, a palatial hall, a church and a harbour and boatyards at Bosham. They probably benefited from their links with the Normans, who had established themselves in Normandy, on the opposite side of the English Channel to Sussex, in the previous century. The buildings at Bosham, at least, played a part in the events leading to the Norman invasion in 1066 and are depicted in the Bayeux tapestry. In September 1066 Harold and his English army defeated one rival claimant to the throne, a Norwegian invader and his army, in Yorkshire, while in the same month another rival, Duke William of Normandy, who also claimed to have been promised the throne by his cousin, the late king, landed an army at Pevensey.

Having landed, Duke William could shelter his forces in the burh and late Roman Saxon shore fort at Pevensey; later, at Hastings (Sussex), his men put up possibly one of the first castles to be seen in Britain. Such a castle, according to its depiction in the Bayeux tapestry, was little more than an earth mound or motte, derived from the upcast dug from an encircling ditch, with a timber watchtower on top; a palisaded enclosure or bailey outside the ditch would shelter most of the men and horses, certainly at night.

It has been claimed that some, at least, of the Norman army also landed near Chichester but there seems to be no clear evidence for this, although it seems likely that the Normans would have wanted to take control of the harbour at Bosham, to secure the means of obtaining further support from Normandy while denying the same facilities to Harold. As for Chichester, if the burh defences were manned the Normans would have had good reason to bypass the town, as they would not have wasted time and effort on investing a walled town at this stage. Their ruthless method of warfare called for a highly mobile field army of mounted knights and foot soldiers, many of them archers, backed up by their new rapidly constructed form of strongpoint, the motte-and-bailey castle. In the event, three weeks later in mid October their forces prevailed against the Anglo-Saxon army, hastily arrived from the north, and Harold was killed. The Normans then burned some towns and villages on their way to the Thames valley, and London and the chief men of the kingdom were intimidated into surrendering. The Normans immediately set about replacing or suborning the Anglo-Saxon political, clerical and land-holding elite, and strengthening the links, already quite strong, between England and Normandy.

Sussex was geographically important; it was the nearest part of England to Normandy, with many coastal harbours, and the site of the invaders' landfall and their victory in battle. A mark of its

---

1 Earl Godwin's chapel at Bosham, as depicted on the Bayeux tapestry
2 Building a motte-and-bailey castle at Hastings (Bayeux tapestry)

strategic importance to the Normans is revealed by the fact that Duke, now King, William entrusted control of western Sussex to one of his most reliable supporters, Roger of Montgomery. The internal divisions of this English shire, now a Norman county, were rationalised and known as rapes; five rapes ran from south to north, each typically with a castle on a navigable river and thus easily accessible from the coast. Chichester and Arundel were at first in the same, westernmost rape, which seems to have been effectively administered at first from Arundel, where Roger built a castle as his main base in the county. Roger of Montgomery was also given the Welsh-English border to secure, which was his main preoccupation.

Taking the Anglo-Saxon title of regional nobility, the king made him Earl of

Shrewsbury, and Montgomery in turn gave his name to a border town and county. In due course Chichester was separated from Arundel and put in its own rape, and a castle was built there. The castle is documented by c 1100, but it is possible that it was built earlier. Probably from well before the Conquest the city had been governed by one or more reeves or a port-reeve on the king's and Earl Godwinson's behalf and appointed by them.

The Church was subject to Norman supremacy just as much as secular institutions in England. Ecclesiastical reorganisation, by which fewer bishops oversaw larger dioceses, led King William in c 1075 to replace the existing minster at Selsey by a new cathedral in Chichester. The cathedral was founded in the south-west quarter of the town, on land already partly in the hands of the Church and partly in the gift of the king. Importantly, the cathedral land ran up

68

to the walls around the whole south-west quadrant, probably the longest single stretch of the walls in a single landholding. In Chichester, unlike some other towns, there was no necessary connection between a landholding immediately inside the walls and management of the corresponding stretch of the walls themselves, but in any case the Church and clerics were generally exempted from obligations to defend the place, or contribute taxes for this purpose. For the time being this probably did not matter, although when the dean wanted to make an opening in the walls to connect his house and garden with his land and orchards outside the walls and running down to the River Lavant, in 1178–80, he had to obtain a licence from the king, and a licence was also required to build a deanery on the wall itself, apparently partly on a bastion overlooking the dean's land outside the walls. (The resulting postern gate is still visible next to the Old Deanery.)

Domesday Book, compiled in 1085–6, compares the value of landholdings then with their value just before the Norman Conquest. Chichester does not appear at the head of the section dealing with Sussex, as the chief town of a county usually does. Instead it is described only as a part of the lands of Earl Roger (ie Roger of Montgomery, Earl of Shrewsbury). In the time of King Edward, before the Conquest, the town is recorded as having contained about 100 plots, each presumably with at least one building on it,

3   Silver penny of William I
4   The Channel coast of Normandy and south-east England, showing the importance of Chichester's location
5   The Norman gateway and motte of Arundel Castle
6   Canon Gate forms the entrance to the Cathedral Close in South Street, Chichester

worth between 6d and 1s each, for a total value of £2 8s 11d. Several burgesses are noted separately, probably living in the north-east quarter of the town, and it has been supposed that the king or the earl (ie the head of the Godwin family) had an official residence in the town, which may have been in the north-west quarter. Twenty years later the plots had been subdivided and 60 more houses had been built. The city appears to have done well by the arrival of the cathedral and the advent of Norman rule. In 1066 the city was worth £15 a year, meaning this was what it could remit annually in taxes, two-thirds to the king and one-third to the earl. By 1086 this was expected to be £25 but the city was actually raising £35 a year. The former Anglo-Saxon landholders, both of property in the town and of manors outside to which the properties were attached, had all been dispossessed.

A castle was built in order to overawe the populace and ensure the king's control of Chichester, as well as to ensure its defence. Almost certainly it was the king who built the castle as Earl Roger had died before 1100, when the castle is first documented, and his lands had temporarily reverted to the crown, his heirs having shown themselves to be much less reliable. The site chosen for the castle was in the north-eastern corner of the town, utilising the existing walls there as an outer enceinte, and possibly an existing mound as the basis for a motte (Chapter 3). The castle motte probably stood above an inner bailey, which was surrounded in turn by a wide almost circular ditch, partly dug to provide material for the motte. The motte could have filled the whole area inside this ditch, but would not necessarily have been any higher as a result. The structure on the motte was of timber, and seems not to have lasted long enough nor been important enough to

have been rebuilt in stone. It is significant that this work did not take the form of any obvious change to the existing defences or improvement of the walls which may, indeed, have been relatively neglected in this period and, except for the stretch immediately beside the castle bailey, been allowed to fall into disrepair and be robbed of useful building stone.

In the castle, the ditch around the inner bailey was continuous, so less reliance was placed on the existing walls, further away. It seems probable that the presence of a castle would have diminished the importance of the walls as a military defence in any case. Walls around a town would always have had a police function, channelling travellers and goods through the gates where they could be inspected and, if necessary, tolls exacted. The castle should have been a much more effective military base than the town walls, but the military usefulness of either a castle or walls would depend crucially on the numbers, equipment and effectiveness of any garrison. In a town like Chichester only the castle would have had a garrison, which would inevitably have had local administrative and political functions, supplementing or overseeing whatever the existing arrangements were, by a bailiff or a reeve. Thus an outer bailey was laid out (approximately under modern Priory Park), which would have been a more public zone. Somewhere in the castle were a prison, documented by the end of the 12th century, and almost certainly a chapel.

---

7   Artist's reconstruction of the motte-and-bailey castle at Chichester (Mike Codd)

8   The remains of the motte in Priory Park

A charter of the reign of Stephen confirms all the rights of a borough and guild merchant (the body of those citizens who held a monopoly of retail trade in a town, except for fairs and market days), which by implication had existed since at least the Norman Conquest. In 1107–8 the bishop was granted the right to hold, and therefore profit from, an annual fair, which was to last for eight days outside the north gate. Other fairs were held outside the east gate. Charters allowed goods to be landed and loaded only at Dell Quay, to ensure that customs dues were paid. The first commodities documented as passing through Chichester's seaport in the early 13th century included wool, bacon and cheese, but goods were obviously traded long before this and customs

due on wool, hides and wool-fells (sheepskins) are frequently mentioned as a group. By 1353 Chichester was one of the staple ports, and possibly the seventh largest port in the country by value. Wine is documented as being imported, presumably from Gascony and Aquitaine (France), which were intermittently in English hands, and by the 15th century the export of wool was replaced by the export of woollen cloth.

Fires damaged the new cathedral and other buildings in the city in 1114 and 1187, while a fire in 1160 damaged the market place, the location and extent of which are uncertain. Considerable property seems to have changed hands in consequence of each

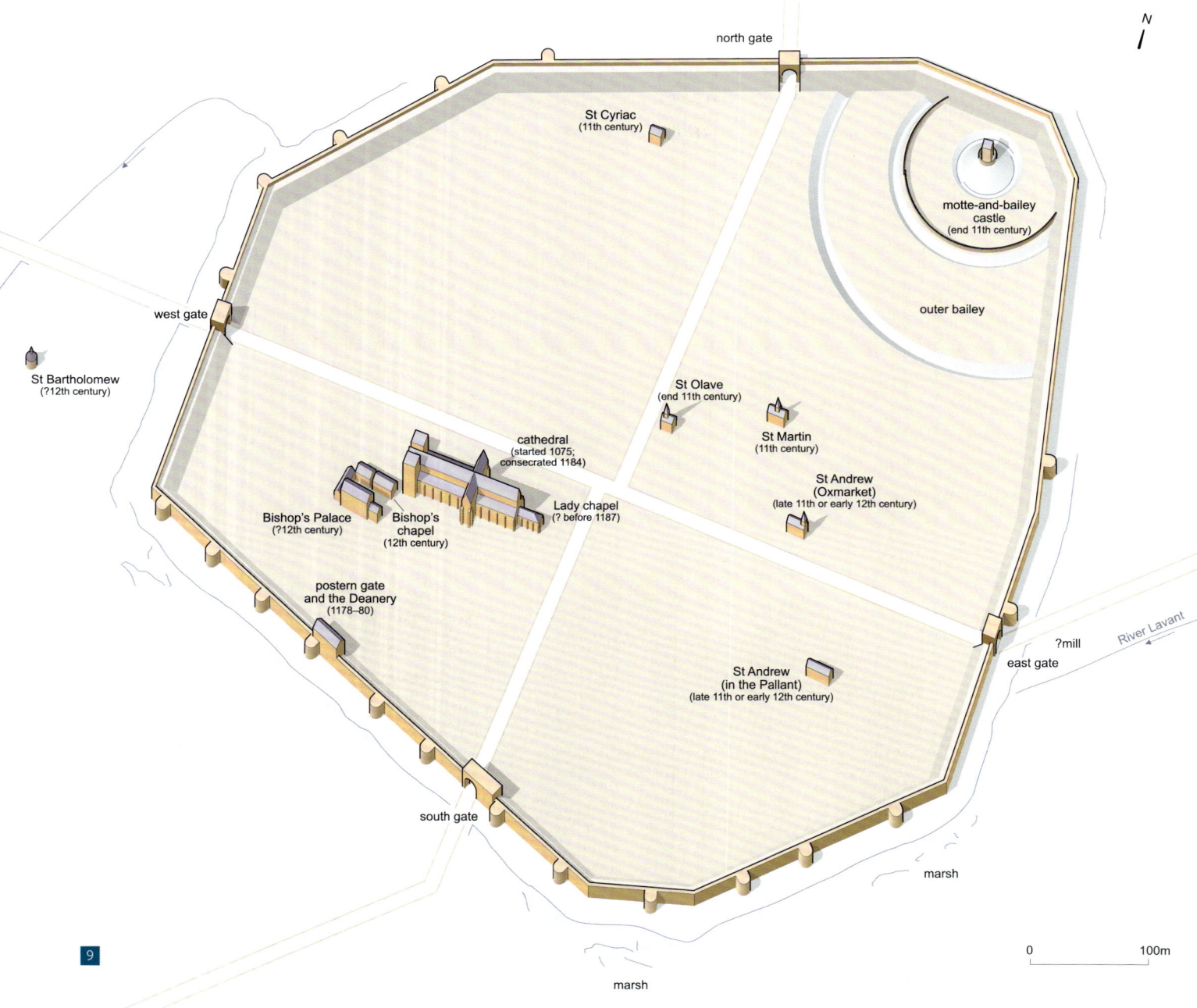

fire, and the fact that Chichester recovered and rebuilt after these fires indicates its economic strength. By 1121 the king, Henry I, had granted the city a charter confirming the existing privileges of the guild merchant and these privileges were confirmed again in 1155 in two charters granted by Henry II to the citizens directly. These charters thus were the first authoritative recognition of the inhabitants as a corporate body.

Walls by their very existence constrained and shaped the capacity of the town to develop. From now on an increase in population would have to be either outside the walls or living and working more densely inside them. But walls could be a military liability as much as an asset, depending on who was able to take advantage of them and man them. Later history shows that they came closest to being demolished (in the 17th century) for the very reason that an enemy force could have taken control of the town when it was not able to be professionally defended and could then, thanks to the walls, have held out against counter-attack (Chapter 8). In the 12th century the walls were not the main defence of

the city so much as the castle, to which the same principles applied. The conflict between noble factions and an ineffective king, John, at the beginning of the 13th century, involved Chichester. In 1204 the king lost control of Normandy to the king of France, who was an opportunistic ally of the English king's domestic enemies and rivals. In the same year one of the king's allies, Simon bishop-elect of Chichester, was given control of the city in return for two palfreys or horses. He ordered all those who owed a duty to contribute to the defence of the city to help in repairing the walls against attack from the king of France. In 1216, when John's opponents were well in the ascendant, a French army landed, captured Chichester castle and occupied the city. However, John died and his successor, Henry III, succeeded the next year in recapturing the castle from the French. The new king promptly ordered Chichester castle to be dismantled.

9   Norman Chichester, 11th–12th centuries

10   Repairing the walls around the castle (Fred van Deelen)

10

7

Medieval wars and uprisings

After the demolition of Chichester castle in 1217–19 the city's only defences were again its walls, which circumstantial evidence suggests were not as effective and up-to-date as they could have been and had probably not been kept in good repair, except for the short stretch around the north-east quadrant that had also protected the castle. Maintenance of a city's walls at this time could be, at least nominally, the duty of a protective overlord, but usually the city had to fund the work corporately. The charters granted to the citizens of Chichester from the 12th century onwards (Chapter 6) usually gave them the farm of the city, that is, the citizens themselves collectively raised the taxes that were

due from the city's inhabitants. In 1226, for instance, this was set at a total of £36 a year. The city could also contribute to aids, which were grants of money to the king that they assessed and collected themselves, whereas tallages, extra tolls on goods and travellers, were assessed externally. The farm excluded, as before, the customs due on wool, hides and sheep-fells as well as on all other imports and exports, which the king's agents therefore were entitled to collect directly. The city was apparently reasonably

---

1 Chichester in the late medieval period, 13th–15th centuries

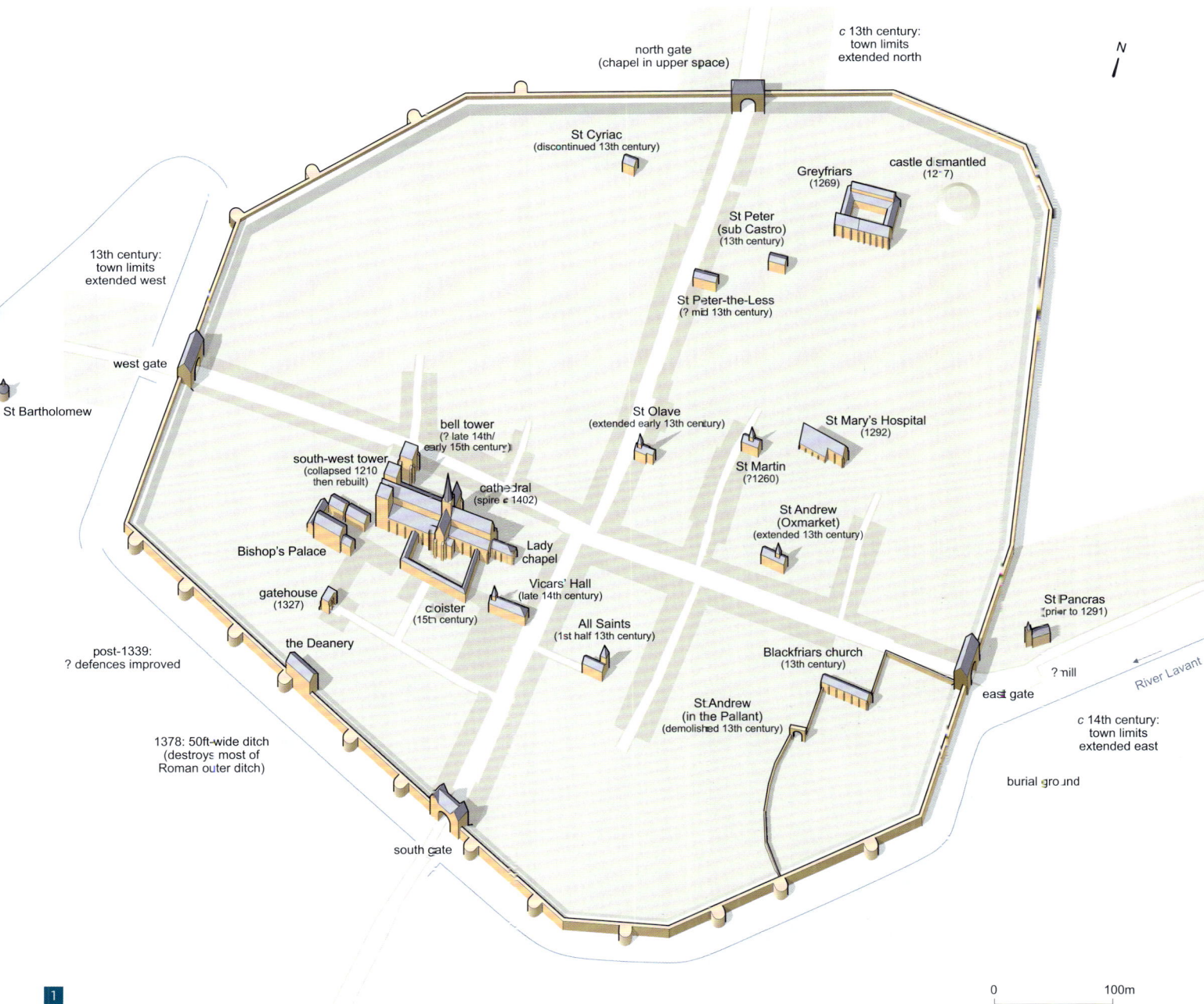

1

prosperous, a though in 1230 the taxes due from the farm were £38 10s in arrears and had been in arrears, it was said, since 1224. In 1227 Henry III gave his brother, Richard Earl of Cornwall and King of the Romans, the right to the proceeds of the city's farm, which presumably implies that Richard was now responsible, among other things, for putting the city's defences in order. In 1261 the king is documented as granting murage to the men of the king of the Romans, meaning that they were empowered to levy additional taxes and tolls for a fixed period in order to finance construction and repair of the walls, although it does not necessarily follow that they actually did this or, if they raised the money, that they spent it properly.

The archaeological evidence for the maintenance of Chichester's walls in this period is scanty and the documentary evidence may be incomplete. Together with the circumstantial evidence that the walls had probably been neglected for some time, the evidence suggests that a considerable reinforcement of the defences was probably put in hand. The best archaeological evidence for medieval work on the upstanding wall is in the north-east quadrant, where drilling (for recent repairs) has determined that the surviving core of the wall is about 2m thick. At some time after the Roman period the outer face of this stretch of the masonry core of the wall was refaced; the excavators plausibly interpreted this refacing as medieval, although it could have been later. Unfortunately this is the very stretch that would have been kept in good repair because it was next to the castle, and it does not allow us to conclude that the rest of the wall was in as good a state as this. Refacing the exposed core would be necessary for its long-term protection from erosion, to prevent an enemy climbing up the wall too easily and to support a crenellated parapet at the top. Without definite evidence for a solid outer face to the wall it is not possible to say that the wall even had a stone parapet or crenellations, but their absence would not have been so unusual. The timber palisades of castles were replaced in stone only as and when military benefit pressed and resources allowed. Timber brattishing, hourds and other structures were still added to the top and outer face of stone walls, towers and gatehouses, and timber walls in the form of park pales were common around emparked tracts of land, for instance, where deer were bred for the sport and table of aristocratic households.

Apparently the ownership of the ditch or ditches in front of the wall around Chichester was in question throughout the 13th century and, as ownership entailed responsibility for its clearance

and recutting, this implies that there was some pressing need to restore the ditch. On the other hand sometimes needs of this kind were invented, and consequently a fine exacted, simply to raise money. Part of the house of one Emeline de Merstone was said to have been built almost in the ditch (*quasi de fossato*) and Emeline was therefore due to pay 1d to the king but, as well as this, she was to pay 18d for the lights on the altar of the Blessed Virgin Mary, presumably in the cathedral. Her house is unlikely to have been built in a fully open ditch. Perhaps it was partly over a portion of the ditch. Perhaps it was on or near Church land; or was this apparently pious exaction simply a way of raising money? In addition, there was a question as to how the responsibilities of the king and the earl were apportioned with respect to the ditch. A ditch (*fossatum*) ran round the outside of the city where the castle had been, in the north-east quadrant, but not around the southern side of the walls where the Church had property. Only the River Lavant was said to flow there. By this time the river probably flowed all the way round the southern half of the walls, from the east gate to the west gate, and powered watermills near both gates. Fresh water was also brought into the city in pipes from springs to the north, the pipes running across the ditch (possibly by a siphon) and through the wall and bank.

Continuing legal complications, reflecting political turmoil, suggest that the state of the city's defences were not improved. The city descended to the king, together with other, much larger benefits held by the earls of Cornwall, such as the honour of Wallingford, a large estate that included the town and castle of Wallingford (Berkshire). The practical benefit of possessing such lands or interest in a city or town was, of course, to receive the rents and other moneys due from them. In 1307, soon after his accession, Edward II gave Chichester and Wallingford to John de Clinton, who two years later was in turn persuaded to give them to the king's favourite, Piers Gaveston. After Gaveston's beheading in 1312 and the reversion of the estates to the king, Edward II gave custody of the city of Chichester to its mayor and citizens, at a reduced farm of £32. As noted in *The Victoria history of the county of Sussex*, at first this gift could be terminated at any time the king pleased, but in 1316, for a payment of 40 marks (or £26 13s 4d), the king renewed the grant to the citizens, and their heirs and successors, with 'the liberties and free customs and all other commodities and profits belonging, by land and water', for a yearly

---

2 **Prosperous Chichester was a thriving medieval market town (Mike Codd)**

fee farm rent of £36. As usual, the king reserved to himself direct collection of customs. By this charter the citizens were given responsibility for administering the city without limit of time or powers. Henceforward the king may have granted the fee farm rent to others, but the citizens had full custody of the city. Custody meant, in practical terms, responsibility for the walls, while the fee farm, a fixed sum raised by the city, was paid to a variety of successive beneficiaries, who held it as a piece of property and had no necessary personal connection with the city. The sum remained fixed, bearing no relation to anything else, and the right to receive it was eventually bought by the city corporation and extinguished. The fee farm in any case bore less and less relation to what the city could actually raise by way of self-assessed taxation nor to what it had to, or could, spend on the walls.

Chichester did not belong to the Cinque Ports, whose jurisdiction went no further west than Seaford (Sussex), some 60km to the east. The Cinque Ports, five ports on the south-eastern seaboard of the country to which other ports were later added or associated, customarily provided medieval kings with naval vessels and crews in return for various privileges such as exemption from taxes. The medieval seas were lawless; a low-level kind of piracy was common, and small-scale, opportunistic raiding on coastal shipping, towns and villages was a constant possibility.

Naval skirmishes and raids by the French on English shipping and coastal towns in 1336 were a foretaste of things to come. When Edward III claimed the French throne in 1337 an era of intermittent war began between England and France. As usual in these circumstances piracy was elevated to the status of honourable warfare by the institution of privateering but, in addition, the French conducted a concerted and unprecedented naval campaign in the English Channel, attacking harbours and towns along the south coast of England and causing much damage and alarm. In the spring of 1338 a small French fleet landed near Portsmouth (Hampshire), an unwalled town and the next important harbour

3

on the English coast 23km west of Chichester. The French burned buildings and boatyards, carried off stores and killed whoever they could find or took them prisoner to ransom them or sell them into slavery. The local militia was unable to muster and offer resistance, nor were any English ships able to pursue the raiders. This dramatic success, revealing English lack of preparation and vulnerability, encouraged French privateers to make hit-and-run attacks all along the south coast. In alliance with Castile and Genoa the French captured Guernsey in the Channel Islands which, in the 13th century, had been the only parts of Normandy that the French had allowed the English to retain. In the autumn of 1338 the French and their allies mounted another major attack, this time on Southampton. Although a walled town, its defences were old and had been left unrepaired. A breach was soon made and Southampton met the same fate as Portsmouth, with huge losses of goods and shipping.

Edward III began a policy of rebuilding fixed defences and constructing warships. An inquisition early in 1339 reported, for example, that at Chichester 'There is no landing place for ships; there are no men of that city who have ships, barges or boats, and no mariners dwell there.' The city was said to be indefensible because the walls had gaps in them, which the citizens could not afford to repair. Thereupon the king appointed the Earl of Arundel, Thomas de Braiose and Master William de Fishbourne to survey the walls and put the city in a state of defence, at the expense of the mayor, bailiffs and citizens. The bishop, dean and chapter agreed to contribute, although they were technically exempt, everyone duly acknowledging that this would not set a precedent. In 1341 the city was allowed to keep £27 of the fee farm payable to the Exchequer, because of the expense of repairing the walls in relation to the city's resources. This was despite the destruction in the previous year of the French fleet in the harbour of Sluys,

4

on the coast of Flanders (now on the modern Belgian-Dutch border), by the English and their Flemish allies. In the event this victory gave the English control of the English Channel, and greatly diminished the threat to England's coastal towns, although this may not have been appreciated at once.

The Bishop of Chichester, Robert de Stratford, in 1340 succeeded his brother, who was archbishop of Canterbury, as Edward's chancellor, responsible for financing the war with France. Unfortunately the treasury was depleted and trade much disturbed, decreasing revenue, but instead the brothers were suspected of not supporting the war as much as they could. The king was forced to dismiss the bishop from the post of chancellor after a few months, but a strange event two years later suggests that the bishop and the war still aroused strong feelings. In 1342 the bishop and former chancellor complained that he had been prevented from entering Chichester and his own cathedral 'by an armed multitude that came out to the suburbs, closing the gates of the city and assaulting, injuring and imprisoning his servants, and extorting fines and ransoms by threats and fear of death' (quoted in The Victoria County History). The bishop accused by name the dean and chapter, most of the city's clergy and numerous laymen, including most of the notable citizens and past

and future members of parliament, but not apparently the mayor. It remains unclear if the bishop was, at that stage, disliked personally or whether the war was disliked by, for instance, the merchants of the city. The ensuing criminal case on the bishop's behalf ended with the outlawry of a single, token layman. This is the only popular disturbance in Chichester known to have made use of the city's gates, despite popular uprisings later in the 14th century and in the 15th century. The dean and chapter of the cathedral, who organised and officiated at its services, were perhaps forced to take sides; the bishop was clearly a political appointment, with which the cathedral officials would not necessarily be in sympathy.

The onset of epidemic plague from c 1348, and English victories in northern France at Crécy (Somme) in 1345 and Poitiers (Vienne) in 1356, led to a truce. When the French resumed the war in 1369 Edward III issued another commission to repair the walls of Chichester, recorded further in The Victoria County History. The mayor and the dean were to co-operate in seeing that the grant of murage for ten years was applied only to these repairs, and all merchants 'who stay there continually and live of their merchandise', even if they had no land or buildings in the city, were to contribute. The king's grant of murage to Chichester in 1370, for nine years, was therefore a continuation and augmentation of the earlier policy of reinforcement of the defences of coastal towns and harbours. In 1377 the king authorised the mayor and bailiffs to complete the city ditch 'newly begun', which was stated to be 50 feet (15.2m) broad, together with the walls, small towers or turrets (turelli) and gates, and to demolish any houses or other buildings either next to the wall or in the way of the broad ditch. Owners of demolished buildings were to be compensated. The mayor was also given the authority to compel all religious as well as secular inhabitants of the city to contribute to the cost. In another grant of murage in 1385 the mayor was given powers to demolish all buildings and cut down all trees within 100 feet (30.5m) of the walls, and to raze suburbs if necessary. For this work the mayor was authorised to order forced labour, impressing people anywhere in the rape of Chichester and

5

5   Robert Sherburne, a later bishop of Chichester, 1508–36
6   The Bishop's Palace gardens, looking towards the cathedral

punishing those who refused. The last recorded grant of murage was in 1443, when the wall in the south-eastern quadrant, between the east gate and the south gate, was to be rebuilt.

The archaeological evidence to bear out the documented repairs to the upstanding structures, and even the digging of a broad ditch, is most exiguous. The defences were not entirely material, either. A chapel of Our Lady upon the north gate is documented in 1374, apparently on the upper floor of the gatehouse. Perhaps this had been recently built in the course of reinforcing the defences. It is possible that the upstanding structures were substantially rebuilt in the late 13th and 14th centuries, perhaps in stages. The exposed Roman core would almost certainly have been refaced, leading to the conclusion that a crenellated parapet in stone would have been reinstated, possibly for the first time since the 4th or 5th centuries AD. More earth, perhaps including upcast from the broad ditch, may have been added to the existing bank to raise it higher and perhaps to support the wall walk, which would by now have been able to occupy no more than half the original width of the Roman-period masonry wall. The gatehouses, if not the gates, would probably have been rebuilt,

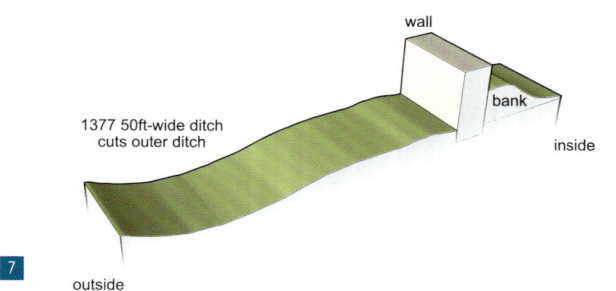

7

too, and are likely to have resembled the surviving 14th-century gatehouse to the Bishop's Palace and the gatehouse to the cathedral precincts, rebuilt in the 16th century, west of South Street. The upper rooms of gatehouses and towers were sometimes let out to tenants, to yield an income for the town, or used for other more communal purposes provided that they could be taken over and used for defence if need arose. Chapels and prisons are commonly found in the gatehouses and towers of city walls. Chichester's prison was over the east gate, although it is uncertain when it was first installed. A medieval town prison did not have to be large, as it was where prisoners were kept in custody before trial, rather than for punishment.

Although there was still plenty of space inside the city walls, by the 14th century suburbs were developing, mainly along the roads to the west and the east, where the churches of St Bartholomew and St Pancras, respectively, were built. Presumably the land was cheaper, or simply available, and the protection of the walls was not important. Bars or movable barriers across the road were often erected beyond the gates and suburbs to stop travellers and exact dues and tolls. Some activities by their very nature found a place outside the walls and especially just outside the gates, such as blacksmithing and farriery and the provision of hostelries and stabling. Acts of parliament of 1252 and 1285 required the gates in town walls to be shut after dark and 'watch and ward' to be kept; watchmen, often the gate-porters, would patrol the night streets and enforce the curfew, the latter meaning minimising fire risk rather than anything more sinister. The town fields, mainly to the east of the city, were also outside the walls, originally cultivated communally or by concession.

7   Schematic section through Chichester's medieval town defences

8   The 14th-century gatehouse to the Bishop's Palace still stands

9   St Pancras church was originally built in the later 13th century and rebuilt in 1750–1 following partial demolition during the Civil War

9

8

Reformation, foreign threats and civil war

The peaceful accession of Henry VIII in 1509 marks, in retrospect, a historical watershed of relevance for Chichester's walls. The continuation of the Tudor dynasty, which had been established by Henry VIII's father after victory in a long-running dynastic civil war, reflected more efficient and effective government, and the relative absence of threats from within that had bedevilled the previous century and a half. New techniques of warfare, especially gunnery, were taken up which, although they had existed before, had not been used much in England. Similarly, the new king was an advocate of a more developed navy, which would make the walls of coastal towns a second, rather than a first, line of defence. Although Henry's foreign policy was essentially one of national self-assertion, even aggrandisement it was the almost accidental circumstances of reformation of the Church that provoked the most serious threats of war.

The Reformation and the imposition of royal supremacy on the English Church in the late 1530s seem not to have affected Chichester particularly severely. The only orders of religious, the two friaries, were suppressed and, in the cathedral, chantry chapels and the shrine of St Richard were destroyed. The saint had been a 13th-century bishop of Chichester whose pious enforcement of ecclesiastical rules and defence of the rights of the Church had resulted in his rapid canonisation. His shrine had been a major attraction for pilgrims, and its destruction, therefore, was felt as an economic as well as possibly a spiritual loss to the city. The two medieval hospitals were revived under Elizabeth

More significant for the safety of the city was the fact that Henry VIII's break with Rome provoked Catholic France and Spain, in

1 Halfgroat of Henry VIII
2 Detail from John Norden's 1595 map of Sussex

This Shire is deuided into 6 Rapes which are distinguished with their letters following,

A The rape of Chichester.
B The rape of Arondell.
C The rape of Bramber.
D The rape of Lewes.
E The rape of Peuensey.
F The rape of Hastinge.

◇ Market townes,
○ Parrishes,
○ Hamletes,
△ Noblemens howses,
○ Howses of gent &c.
▲ Castles
◘ Religious places,
○ Chappells,
▲ Beackens,

Iodes Norden deliniauit anno 1595.
Christof. Shwytzer sculp

1538, to enter into an anti-English alliance. Faced with the threat of invasion from two of the most powerful countries in Europe, Henry VIII had new forts constructed, mainly along the coast of Kent and the south-west of England. These so-called device forts were for all practical purposes small, compact, masonry platforms for heavy guns. A renewed threat of war with France in 1544 led to more of these forts being constructed around the Solent. The nearest of these forts to Chichester were at Camber (Sussex), protecting Rye and Winchelsea at the opposite end of Sussex, more than 100km to the east, and at Southsea (Hampshire), on the point of the Portsmouth promontory, 22km to the west. The fort at Camber had been begun in 1510, but was updated later. The design and armament of these forts reflected both the use of artillery of continually increasing technical sophistication, reliability and power, and an underlying appreciation of the value of a forward seaborne defence by means of warships carrying guns, with trained crews. Both these developments would eventually render the walls of Chichester obsolete in a military sense.

Despite the fact that the defences must have been maintained to some degree during the war scares of Henry VIII's reign, an accident soon afterwards indicates how unstable they really were. In November 1553 a coroner's inquest recorded that a coroner empanelled 14 men as an inquest jury to hear how the wall had caused the death of two children: 'At one o'clock on 2nd November ... Richard Stone, aged over four, and Joan Middleton, aged three, both of Chichester, were sitting and playing under the north wall of the city when, through the force of the wind part of the wall, to a length of 60 feet [18.3m], collapsed and four cartloads of stones fell on them and buried them.' Presumably it was the facing and perhaps the crenellated parapet of the upstanding wall that collapsed.

Chichester harbour was silting up, like similarly long-established ports to the east, and becoming less practicable for larger vessels. The Chichester Haven Act of 1584 envisaged widening Chichester harbour and dredging a canal up to the west gate of the city. A canal was felt to be needed because there were no warehouses at Dell Quay and the road between there and the city was in disrepair. In the event nothing was actually built, perhaps because of the attempt by the Spanish fleet to invade England in 1588.

To fight the Spanish Armada Chichester paid for a ship of 70 tons (71.1 metric tons), with a crew of 50, and gun batteries were installed at the entrance to Chichester harbour at Cakeham, Selsey and Pagham. This was, in effect, an updating of the Henrician defence of the coast, and suggests that Chichester was not regarded as likely to be a major target itself for an enemy. The city was vulnerable mainly because it was not far inland from the head of a shallow harbour and near numerous other possible landing places for an invader.

In 1596, a few years after the defeat at sea of the armada, an anonymous petition was sent to the Lord Treasurer of England. The tone, naturally, is one of complaint. The petitioner attributes the decay of the city to the poor, who are said to be driving out the 'better sort' of inhabitants. More to the point, the petitioner complains of the poor state of the city's walls:
thieves which robbed in the country have thence fled by night to hide themselves in the city, and thieves that robbed in the city have easily from thence conveyed themselves into the country by reason the city walls are greatly decayed. … Then rest I heartily wishing that the citizens were ordered to maintain much better the gates, walls and rampiers [ramparts] of the city.
Half the fee farm of about £120 per annum ought to be devoted to the upkeep of the walls. For good measure the petitioner adds that the ancient methods of buying and selling in the city should be restored, probably a reference to the guilds which by then were more or less in desuetude, and the 'good harbour, not 5km away, ought to shelter 300 sail of ships of 100 or 150 tons [101.6 or 152.4 metric tons] apiece'.

Early in the 17th century, war with France and Spain was again a possibility, and as war appeared more or less likely so defensive measures were made more stringent or were relaxed. This became mixed up with the need to keep trained soldiers on hand, the king's chronic shortage of money to pay for their keep, and a growing conflict between the country's political class represented in parliament and the king's assertion of an absolute right to rule. In 1628, for instance, as recounted in The Victoria County History, some 200 soldiers were billeted in the rape and city of Chichester, which was considered by the inhabitants to be especially burdensome as they were already 'full freight with soldiers'. In 1634 the king ordered the city of Chichester, with other towns in Sussex and Kent, to pay for a warship of 800 tons (812.8 metric tons) and its crew of 260 men (much larger than the ship of 1588), with all necessary munitions and victuals. For the first levy of ship money the city was assessed at £150, but for the second the assessment was reduced by nearly half, to £77 7s 4d. The imposition of ship money on towns across the whole country, without parliamentary sanction, was widely resented. We might have expected the taxpayers of Chichester, as a coastal city that should have benefited from the expense of providing warships being shared in this way, to have been in favour of ship money, but in fact of all the coastal towns of Sussex only Hastings approved. The government was informed that, at Chichester, ship money was unpaid and the soldiers were unruly.

The population of Chichester, like much of the country, was divided between supporters of the king and those of parliament, although we can imagine that many preferred not to have to choose until the king's call to arms in 1642 forced the matter. Political loyalty was also, confusingly to our eyes, mixed up with religious loyalty, as the existence of a national religion endorsed by the state to which everyone would belong was still a ruling assumption of public life. In Chichester it is thought that the most prominent citizens and merchants were generally sympathetic to parliament, and some of them may even have been puritans in religious doctrine, while the numerous clerical population of this cathedral city was sympathetic to the king. The country gentry of the region, some of whom had houses and property in the city as well as large estates outside, were also in general Royalist; some notable families were still Catholic (and consequently subject to recurrent fines).

3 The earliest known town plan of Chichester, created by John Norden in 1595

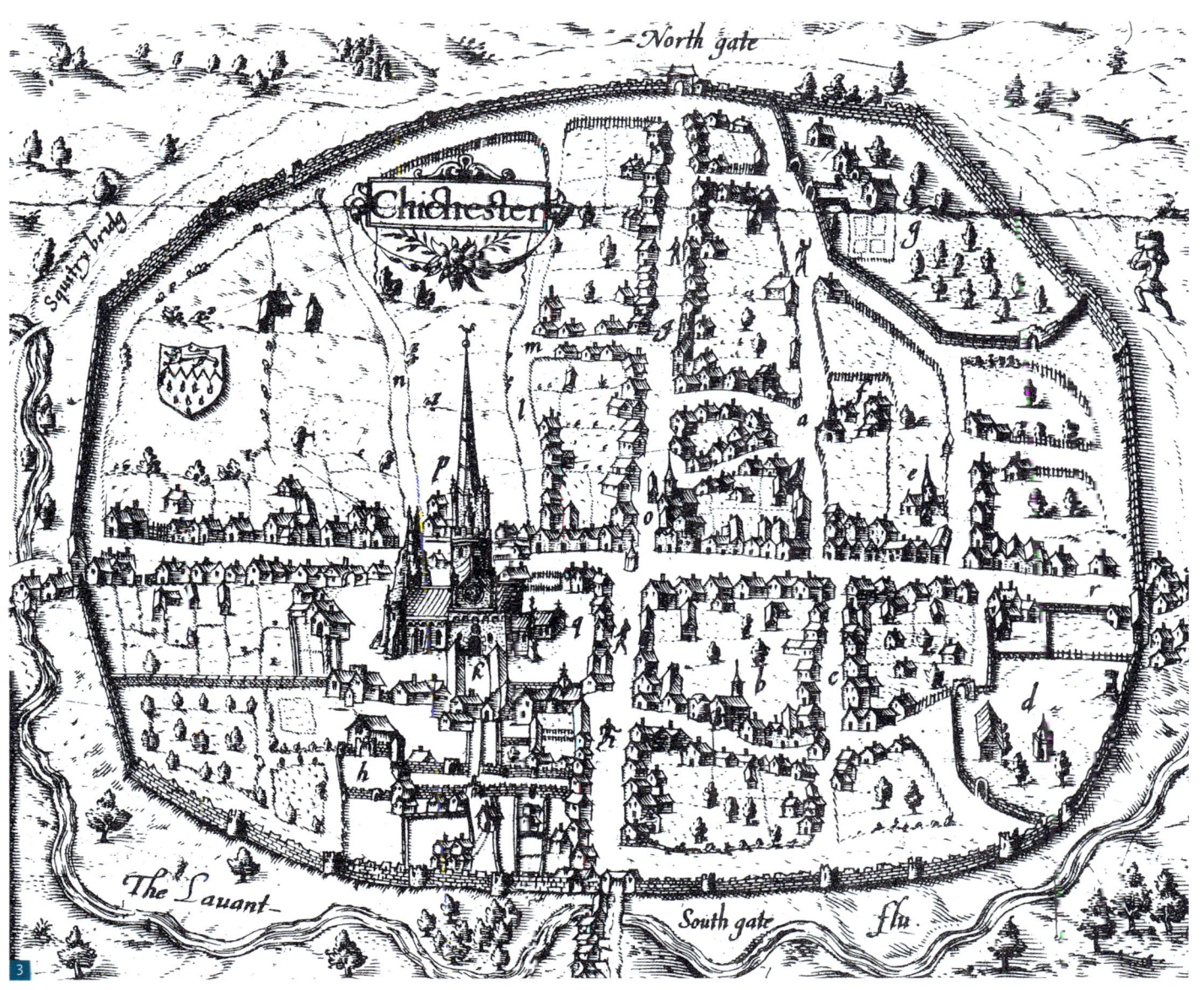

 (within map) North gate · Chichester · Squtry brig · The Lauant · South gate · flu.

In the Civil War the strategic importance of Chichester lay not in itself but in its sheltered harbour and in its position in relation both to Portsmouth, already an important naval station, to the west, and to London, which was Parliament's base, to the north-east. In Parliament's organisation of its war effort, Chichester was regarded as belonging to the 'western parts' and was put under the Committee for the West. The Sussex gentry tried to persuade the king, whose base was at Oxford, to take control of Chichester and from there launch operations westwards, but the king had almost as many options as supporters and could not satisfy them all. In August 1642 some leading citizens of Chichester issued what they called a 'valiant resolution', declaring their

determination to stand for the rights of parliament, the Protestant religion, the laws of the land and the liberty of the people. In response the mayor gave out a royal proclamation, a commission of array, calling upon all able-bodied men to take up arms for the king. Despite the support of the bishop, the recorder or magistrate, who was also a member of parliament, and others, the mayor felt it was too dangerous to stay and he left the city to join the king himself.

His successor acceded to a kind of Royalist coup in the city. The main leader of the Parliamentary faction, William Cawley, had called his supporters to the town hall, in Greyfriars. The mayor

proposed that 20 citizens and 20 gentlemen should jointly keep watch on the gates and walls, but Sir John Morley of Halnaker appeared with 30 gentlemen and 50 others and, refusing to send them away, threatened the mayor and seized the keys of the gates. On 16 December 1642, with 200 of the county militia and guns taken from Portsmouth, the sheriff of the county, Sir Edward Ford, entered Chichester and imprisoned some of the Parliamentary

faction Meanwhile a Parliamentary army led by Sir William Waller, which had already taken Farnham (Surrey), Winchester and Arundel, was advancing on Chichester. On 22 December Waller's army took up position just north of the city, and began a siege.

According to Waller's own account, published later, his plan was to attack the northern, eastern and western defences of the city in turn. His account is illustrated with a plan view that shows outworks of some kind extending to the east of the city walls in the suburb of St Pancras. These appear to have been banks of earth, dug from ditches just in front and laid out on a simple rectangular plan, forming what contemporaries would have called a bulwark or sconce, to shelter guns that could fire on the approaches to the main defensive works. The implication is that before Waller's force arrived the Royalist defenders had managed to dig ditches and throw up these earthworks to command the approach to the city from the direction of Arundel. In addition, the Royalists are said to have themselves burned down some of

5

6

7

4   Chichester at the time of the Civil War

5   Sir William Waller

6   A harquebusier, a lightly armed horse soldier; the harquebus was the short firearm they carried

7   Civil War armour – from left: breast plate; early 1640s helmet worn by a harquebusier; 1640s helmet, which would originally have had cheek-pieces and a sliding nasal bar to protect the face

the buildings in the eastern suburb, probably to deny their use as cover to the besiegers. As well as these outworks, a relatively narrow ditch seems to have been dug around the outside of, and quite close to, the city walls. This ditch has been seen in excavations several times, mainly around the southern half of the circuit of the walls, but its mid 17th-century date has only recently been confirmed. The military value of this ditch would seem to have been rather slight, and it is possible that it post-dates the siege (below).

The besiegers and defenders faced each other at first over the northern part of the city walls. The Royalists fired their guns from the north wall and made a sortie through the north gate, which Waller's army easily repulsed. Waller set up his guns at the Broyle and, after the Royalists refused to surrender to him, began firing. At first the Parliamentary force's guns overshot the city, but later they were able to fire over, or possibly through, the north gate to hit the crossroads in the centre of the city. Waller's forces captured and burned the western suburbs, including the church of St Bartholomew, while many buildings in the eastern suburbs were burned by the Royalists. They did not destroy the church of St

Pancras, though, from the tower of which Parliamentary soldiers were able to shoot down on the city. By 28 December the Parliamentary forces had taken up positions on the south side of the city and were making very visible preparations to simultaneously bombard the west and east gates and the small postern gate next to the Deanery, on the south. This narrow postern was walled up, but the blocking was said to have been only one brick thick. The Deanery had been rebuilt earlier in the 17th century (the rectangular base of this, now called the Old Deanery, survives projecting from the line of the wall). On 29 December, before the Parliamentary attacks began, the Royalist garrison in the city surrendered on terms of 'quarter and honourable usage', that is, they would merely be disarmed, fined and allowed to go home. In fact the Royalist gentlemen were left with practically only the clothes they stood up in, according to the eyewitness account of the dean, and the cathedral was badly damaged by rampaging Parliamentary soldiers, whom Waller could not, or would not, restrain.

As a result of the siege the medieval Deanery on the south wall was in ruins, the gates and gatehouses were presumably damaged,

8

and the western and eastern suburbs devastated. Chichester seems to have seen no more action in the war. Waller was made a major general in charge of Sussex, Surrey, Hampshire and Kent. Cawley was appointed governor of Chichester. (A few years later, Cawley was to be one of the signatories of the king's death warrant and he eventually died in exile in Protestant Switzerland.) Like others before him, Cawley had difficulty meeting the demands of higher authority for money and men; of £4000 required, only £100 could be raised, and of 67 men impressed in the rape of Chichester, only 27 could be found. Both in the city and in the surrounding villages people who wanted the war and its depredations to end formed what were called 'clubs'. Their members, or clubmen, gathered by the hundred at pre-arranged spots to make a visible protest.

In 1648 a renewed attempt at a Royalist takeover of the city was foiled. Charles I's trial and execution in 1649 did not mark an end to the conflict. In 1651 his heir, Charles II, after the defeat of his remaining English forces and their Scottish allies at Worcester, was forced for his life to flee the country secretly. Royalist and Catholic families gave him shelter and, passing through Sussex, he was eventually able to leave for France from Shoreham.

The narrow ditch that ran around the walls and bastions has been found to contain, where it was excavated recently in the south-west quadrant, objects of 17th-century date, such as clay tobacco pipes and pottery. These indicate that the ditch is associated with the period of the Civil War, but they cannot be dated precisely enough for us to be able to say if the ditch was dug before the siege in 1642 or afterwards. A ditch could have been dug after the siege in order to protect the city in case of any further attack. A possible military purpose of the ditch may have been to bank up earth in front of the masonry wall, at its

base, to absorb the shock of cannon balls and mortars fired from some distance away. Perhaps the ditch was also intended to mark a kind of deadline, so citizens and others would go no nearer the outer face of the wall than the line of the ditch. This would have preserved the masonry in the wall from being robbed. A cannon ball has, in any case, been recovered from the outer face of the wall in the north-eastern sector. Recent excavations and observations suggest that much of the damage was done during the Civil War and the subsequent period of the Commonwealth, and the most uncertainty and difficulty may have been experienced towards the end of this period, in the late 1650s.

By 1659, when Parliament's military government had lost much of its moral and political authority, and popular support, secret negotiations began to restore Charles II to the throne on suitable terms. Among many other alarms and suspicions, it was feared that a Royalist attack from France was to be made on Chichester. A French 'plan de Chichester' of c 1650 may be inaccurate but its very existence shows that some preparations were made. To defend the coast of west Sussex 2000 soldiers were sent to the area, naval defences were set up and an order to demolish the city walls of Chichester was issued, possibly by the city's governor. In the event, no attack came, and the walls were spared.

8　Waller's army attacking the east gate (Fred van Deelen)

9　The cannon ball as discovered embedded in the bank behind the modern wall

9

9

Prosperity and gentility

After the end of the Civil War and the restoration of Charles II to the throne in 1660, it was clear that the country's defence depended on its navy more than anything else and town walls such as those of Chichester, were rapidly losing military effectiveness. A new factor was entering into consideration, however, which can be summed up as the public amenity value of the walls. Both these factors, the residual and diminishing military value and the fashionable and growing public amenity value, played a part in the survival and maintenance of the walls at the end of the 17th and for much of the 18th centuries.

Coincidentally, Chichester city council's minutes are preserved from 1685 onwards. The city council met every week or two, and its minutes record the fairly intermittent attention paid to the walls, such items taking up perhaps 1–2% of the council's agenda. The mayor was generally charged with immediate responsibility for seeing that the council's decisions were carried out. On 22 February 1688, for instance, the council 'ordered that Mr Mayor do take care to have the wall of this city mended and the charge shall be allowed him …'. The background to this order was almost certainly the Catholic policies of James II, the younger brother of Charles II who had succeeded to the throne on Charles's death in 1685. The new king's vigorous promotion of Catholicism threatened to renew the conflict of the previous generation, for he was supported by France, while the Protestant opposition to him was supported by the Netherlands, and either country might have been expected to intervene. The political class in England was divided between those loyal to the king who favoured a strict line of succession (Tories) and those loyal to the king who nevertheless favoured a Protestant succession (Whigs). There were also those more extreme Protestants not loyal to the king who supported the claim to the throne of the Duke of Monmouth, the illegitimate son of Charles I, and there were many of this persuasion in Chichester, but Monmouth's attempt to take the throne by force in 1685 had failed abjectly and his adherents were subjected to draconian punishment. The birth of a male heir

to James II in 1688 precipitated a crisis, for this child, who was expected to be brought up a Catholic, would take precedence over his older sisters, who had both been raised as Protestants. The older sister, Mary, the next legitimate Protestant in line, and her husband (who was also her cousin), William of Orange, the Dutch stadtholder, landed in England with a small army; James II fled the country (on his second attempt), in effect abdicating. Negotiations between parliament, on the one hand, and Mary and her husband on the other ended with agreement that Mary and William would both reign jointly, largely on parliament's terms.

If war did not threaten, then Chichester council would be concerned with the city's walls only when something urgently demanded their attention, such as when disrepair threatened to bring the upstanding wall down, or else they were concerned in a more routine way when, for example, they had to confirm the renewal of leases of houses and gardens along the inside of the wall and bank. All these matters are of interest to us because they probably represent what the city had to consider in earlier times, too, the records of which do not survive or were never made. In a procedure typical of many cases to do with the walls, the council would order that a certain number of the council's members would view the place in question and then either report back or, less often make a decision themselves. Thus on 7 March 1688 the council 'ordered . . [that two or more named members] do survey the city wall adjoining to a garden now in the occupation of Edward Lawson [at South Walls, in the south-east quadrant] and to report to the next house [ie council meeting] in what condition the same now is as to repairs.' A week later Lawson's lease was confirmed, explicitly stating he was not to have to 'mend or ready in repair' the city walls beside his garden. Tenants were frequently concerned that the terms of their tenancies should exclude responsibility for the walls.

---

1 View of Chichester from the north, 1724

People encroached on the city's land, probably along the inside of the walls. On 29 April 1698 the council was told that a 'Mr Lilhieff in building his barn at the East Walls hath made an incroachment of 538 foot [164m] in length and 5 foot [1.5m] in breadth' and 'at the Cockspit being 42 foot [12.8m] in length and a foot and a half [0.5m] in breadth.' All the council could practicably do was fine the man and force him to take a lease on the land in question. Leased properties that abutted or stood on the bank include stables and a malthouse at South Walls, stables under the North Walls, and several cottages, gardens, orchards and barns. Most of these seem to have been in the south-east quadrant of the circuit or as minuted on 22 January 1738, on 'the inner rampier [bank] of the South Wall.' Renewal of leases was made on payment of a fine, meaning a fee, which as recorded on 5 January 1710 could sometimes be 'ten bottles of wine' or '1s[hilling] and six bottles of wine'. To judge by arrangements made for celebrating royal events, the 30 or so council members liked their wine, and they often held council meetings in the mayor's house or, if not there, then in a suitable inn, such as the Swan in East Street.

The first mention of any part of the walls being used as a public amenity comes indirectly, in 1719. The council ordered on 4 September that Dell Quay be dug deeper 'for the more sure having water here in dry times' and the gravel produced was to be laid 'where tis wanting on the north walls to make the walk there level'; as usual, the mayor was to see to this. On 20 January 1721 the council 'ordered that the north walls be repaired, that trees be planted in such places as are wanting and that the walks be new gravelled at the discretion of Mr Mayor …', the Steward of the city paying the costs. This probably refers to a walk along the top of the bank, rather than the masonry wall itself, in the north-west quadrant. Only a few houses existed outside the walls there, near the west gate, and the view outwards would have been of fields, meadows and woodland, and the Downs beyond, while the view inland would have looked across relatively open ground, orchards and gardens, towards the roofs of houses and the spire and the bell tower of the cathedral. Fashionable private gardens had contained mounts in the 17th century, from which one could admire the rest of the garden laid out below and also take in a borrowed view beyond. In Chichester itself, the city wall and bank around the west and south sides of the garden of the Bishop's Palace was already such a raised walk. By laying out a footpath on other stretches of the upstanding wall and bank to

2 The raised walk inside the wall along the south-west quadrant, within the Bishop's Palace garden

3 A detail from Samuel and Nathaniel Buck's 1738 view across the Westgate fields towards the cathedral

2

which the citizens had access, the council was probably meeting a demand from those of its inhabitants with the leisure and interest to promenade there. Perhaps some members of the council, or their families and visitors, liked to take the air and take in the view on a fine day. Perhaps it was argued that the council was minimising its liability for the safety of anyone who walked on the walls. In any case a pleasant walk along the walls could be regarded as a civic asset.

Other cities and towns, too, were exploiting otherwise problematical sites in this way, laying out pleasant walks. There were early examples: Exeter (Devon), where parts of the walls were made into a public promenade in the 17th century; Chester (Cheshire), where the city council had flag stones laid on the walls for a public promenade in 1707; Dorchester (Dorset) where, although the masonry wall was largely robbed, the municipal authorities levelled the top of the remaining bank in about 1712 and planted trees along it to form the Walks; Shrewsbury (Shropshire), where a public garden was laid out in 1719 in the Quarry, between the town walls and a bend of the River Severn; Hereford (Herefordshire), where the Sally Walk was laid out along a portion of the walls in the 18th century; and Canterbury, where an enterprising local councillor made a garden of the Dane John and adjacent city walls in 1790–3. If this kind of town walk or garden was created by private initiative, it was usual for visitors to have to pay to enter. If a place of public resort was also free of charge, it was probably because charging a fee was unfeasible. Probably the latter was the case at Chichester's walls.

Urban pleasure gardens open to the paying public were a well-established phenomenon by the 18th century, especially on the outskirts of London or attached to taverns and rural watering places, complete with music, eating and drinking, dancing and simple pastimes like bowls and skittles. Economically and culturally, people who were content to simply walk and admire their surroundings and, perhaps, see and be seen, were a socially select minority. In London, Charles II, the pacemaker of fashion, had opened the royal parks to the public, but it was probably understood that this was still a select public, or at least a socially highly segregated public. Elsewhere, visiting the parks and landscaped estates of great country houses had become a fashionable thing to do by the 18th century. Visitors were not expected to be on social terms with the people of the house; they simply introduced themselves to a porter or lodge-keeper and, if admitted, would spend an hour or two in the grounds and then, on their way out, leave a tip if they liked. Only a minority could possibly have done this kind of visiting. In early 18th-century Chichester, for example, visitors to the garden of Sir Hutchin Williams's new house at Priory Park would have been able to see the north-east quadrant of the walls from inside the city, as visitors to the gardens of the Bishop's Palace would have seen the south-west quadrant. By contrast, no payment was required to walk on North Walls, and the footpath was apparently

4 Promenaders at Priory Park (Fred van Deelen)
5 Postcard showing the wall walk along the north-east quadrant
6 The same view remains little changed today

4

96

City Walls from East, Chichester

5

6

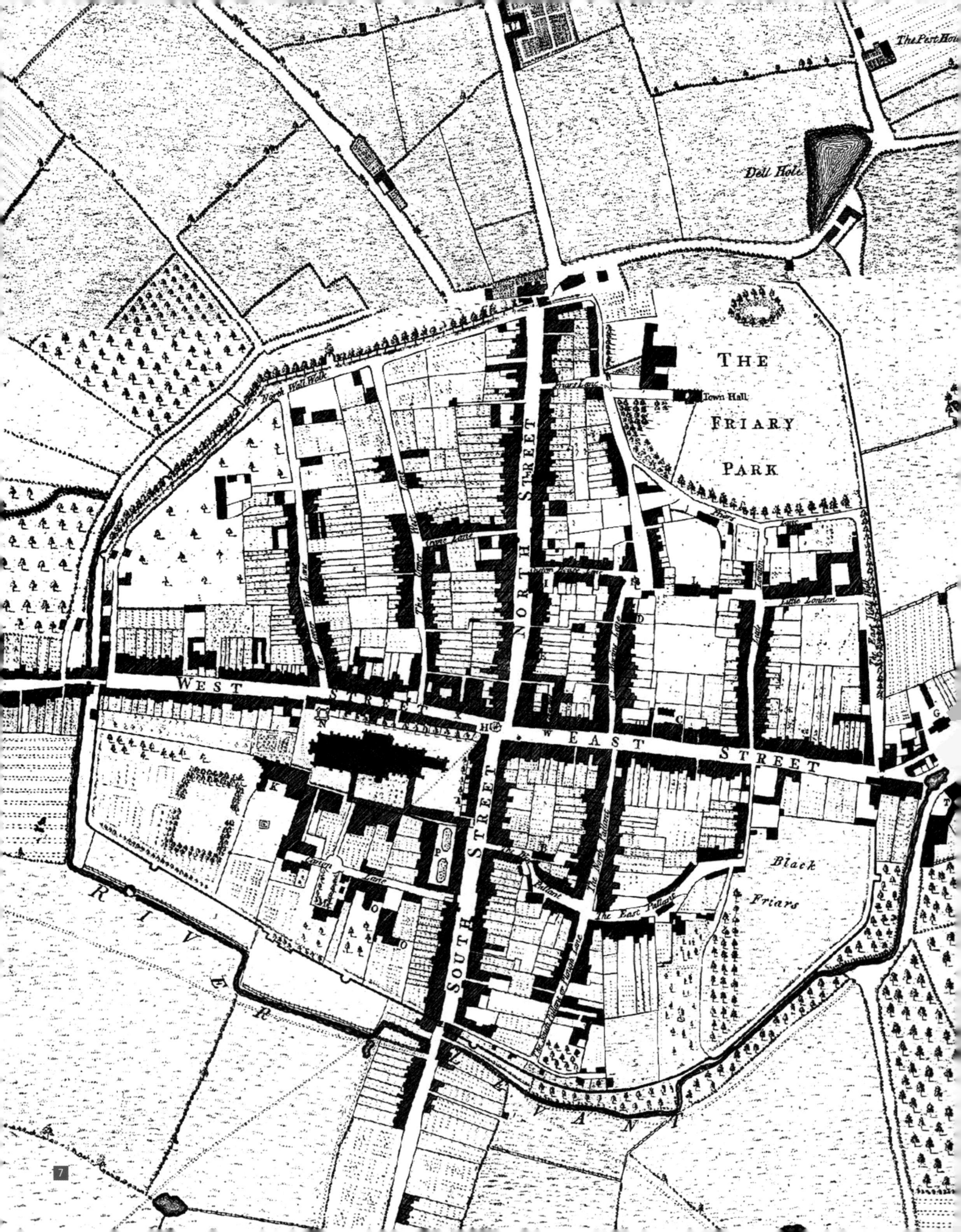

THE PEST HOUSE

Dell Hole

THE
FRIARY
PARK

Town Hall

Friars Lane

NORTH STREET

North Wall Walk

Love Lane

Little London

WEST
STREET
THE SHAMBLES

EAST
STREET

C

SOUTH STREET

RIVER

Black
Friars

The North Pallant
The East Pallant

7

open to anyone at any time. In this sense the public walk on the walls would have been like any other public footpath or right of way. It was not agreed until 13 November 1777 that the council would build 'proper steps and a hand rail' between the walk on North Walls and the Lower West Lane. On 8 March 1779 the council decided to construct steps to ascend 'the ramparts of the East Walls … against the lane called Little London', and on 17 January 1788 it was minuted that the North Walls ramparts were to be 'new planked' and the walk regravelled. Planking may have been to retain the bank. It was recorded on 29 September 1785 that the council bought two stone rollers for the gravel paths and, on 6 April 1825, these were replaced by two iron rollers.

The discovery in 1723 of the inscription referring, as was thought, to Cogidumnus (Chapter 2) could only have aroused great antiquarian interest in the city and increased civic pride. In that age every educated person would have known their Tacitus, or would have liked to appear to know, and many would have recognised at once the historical context of the inscription. It was not something remote. The inscription itself was set up in a kind of temple in the grounds of Goodwood, the seat of Chichester's patron, the Duke of Richmond (and has since been moved to the porch of Chichester's Council House in North Street). John Aubrey, the antiquary, recording his impressions of the city in c 1670, mentions what he takes to be Roman camps north of the city, probably the earthworks of Chichester dykes and other features, but does not mention the city and its walls as necessarily ancient. By contrast, the Revd Jeremiah Miles, Dean of Exeter, writing in 1743 avers that 'Chichester was doubtless a Roman town; ye Roman inscription wch was dug up there some few years ago is a convincing proof of it; & that there was in it a Temple dedicated to Neptune, & Minerva It could be no other place but Regnum of the [Antonine] Itinerary.' (Identifying Roman Chichester's name is discussed in Chapter 10.)

Elsewhere the walls in the city's care still performed various other functions apart, residually, from defence. On 10 February 1743 the council approved estimates for 'carpenter's and bricklayer's work for building a hovel at the East Walls for housing the sheep walks and trucks, and coping the said walls'. The location, near East Street where animals were penned in the fortnightly livestock market, suggests that these walks and trucks were equipment for the market. On 20 June 1744 the council agreed that, at the east gate, the 'Keeper of the Goal [sic] of the city' could occupy a house next to the east gate and the 'goal', 'wherein the porter of the gate hath lately dwelt' (remarkably, the word 'gaol' is consistently

misspelled in the council's minutes throughout the 18th century). At the same time the council decided to retire the porter of the south gate 'by reason of his great age and infirmities' and replace him by, presumably, a younger and fitter man. Minor posts such as this, in the gift of a municipal body, when they fell vacant would often be claimed by deserving relatives of the last post-holder, and in the 18th century some could come to be regarded as practically hereditary. In normal times such men as gate-porters might keep the gate open by day and patrol the streets by night, in furtherance of a town's responsibility for 'watch and ward'. Since the 13th century the law had required walled towns to shut their gates after dark and observe a curfew. This also applied to towns that had gates, even if they had no walls. In later centuries the porter was the person who, if a late traveller was lucky would open a gate and probably expect to be paid a fee or a tip for his trouble.

On 13 June 1754 the city seems to have hit on a way of making repair of the city walls almost self-financing. In company with the city carpenter and the city bricklayer, six members of the council were ordered to view Dell Quay and part of East Walls, which were said to be 'in great decay for want of repair and, unless speedily repaired, in danger of falling and becoming a great charge and expense to rebuild.' The mayor also said that 'the rampier or bank of the north walls … and walk thereon [were] broke down in many places and much out of repair.' He evidently made the suggestion that 'every other of the trees now on the said rampier … be cut down and sold for the best price … and the monies arriving thereby [be] applied towards repairing the said rampier … to make the walk safe and convenient'. Four days later the council accepted the city bricklayer's estimate for repair of the East Walls of £11 15s. It was not for another five months, minuted on 29 November, that the six council members got round to their viewing of the trees, by then bare, to decide which to cut down and what their value would be, and at the next meeting on 5 December they reported that they had marked 29 trees for felling. Unfortunately we do not know how much this timber was sold for, nor whether it did cover the expenses of repair, but the same expedient was used again, recorded on 27 January 1774, 8 March 1779 and 4 March 1780, when new trees had grown. Other sources could sometimes be tapped. When in 1771, the mayor, five council members and the city bricklayer reported that the wall was in poor condition, especially south of the west gate and at East Walls, it was said that £170 remained of 'moneys lately

7 Plan of Chichester in 1769 by William Gardner

given' by the city's two MPs 'as a benefaction for the public utility of the … city.' The council agreed on 11 June, firstly, to spend this on moving a conduit and then to spend the surplus on 'widening and rendering most commodious the walk or terrace upon the north walls … as far as the same moneys will extend'. Some of this money may have gone on refacing in brick the stretch of the upstanding wall south of the west gate, backing on to the west side of the garden of the Bishop's Palace. On 12 May 1772 the city bricklayer's bill of £36 5s 5d for repair of the walls was passed for payment, perhaps referring to this brickwork. The wall on the south side of the garden, facing on to the land of the dean's farm, was the responsibility of the dean rather than the bishop and may have been treated differently for that reason, if no other. It may seem odd that this portion of the masonry wall was rebuilt in brick, at such expense, but this may have been in order for the new wall to serve better as a garden wall, retaining and reradiating the heat of the sun to ripen soft fruit, such as apricots, figs and plums, planted directly in front of it. (The wall, now facing on to the pavement along Avenue de Chartres, is still noticeably warm on a sunny day.)

On 2 October 1773 the council approved a request to make a 'postern or passage four feet [1.2m] wide' through the wall and bank north of the east gate, in lieu of a fine for renewing a lease on property next to the wall and provided that the work was 'to the design and estimate' of the city bricklayer and the city carpenter. The opening was to connect two properties in the same ownership but on different sides of the wall. This must have been duly carried out. The talk of making openings through the wall may have set the council members thinking, or perhaps the gate-porters had outlived their usefulness. Less than three weeks later the council

decided on 20 October that removing all four gates 'will be of great convenience and utility to the citizens and others passing to and from the city' and ordered 'that such gates and buildings be taken down … as soon as … can be conveniently done beginning with the … north gate'. This was also largely self-financing, for the council further ordered that 'the materials of such gates be sold to defray the expenses of taking down.' Less than two months later on 16 December, the council was considering widening the road from North Street to the Broyle, outside the walls, and was ready to pay compensation for land taken 'on the east side of the ground where the north gate lately stood'. The proposed new edge of the road was already staked out, but the work could not proceed at once because the occupant of the ground, a Mrs Rogers, not the landowner, was holding out for compensation, too. The council, five weeks later, agreed on 27 January 1774 to build her a new oven at their expense. Within another four months, minuted on 9 May 1774, the west and south gates had gone, 'the timber and stones' of all three demolished gates to be 'forthwith sold by auction to the highest bidder'. Not only that, the council then approved another request to make a passage through the 'rampier or wall' somewhere else unspecified. The east gate, in which the city had its prison, was not demolished until 1783, when a new prison had been built not far away outside the walls. It may have been the imminent disappearance of this gate that prompted Grimm to draw it, apparently looking west from outside.

8   Late 18th-century brick facing to the wall around the Bishop's Palace garden

9   Grimm's view of the outside of the east gate in 1782, just before demolition (the inscription on it is incorrect)

8

N.E. Side of the W. Gate at Chichester.

9

Towards the end of the 18th century the council was approving requests for bastions to be taken down, provided that all damage to the upstanding wall was made good. Some locations can only be identified by the name of the person making the request; on 30 March 1780, for example, someone wanted to remove a bastion that was projecting into his garden, and on 3 November 1807 Henry Souter wanted to demolish a bastion at the south-west end of North Walls. Not everyone wanted bastions removed, however. At Price's Yard, in the south-east quadrant, not only was a bastion added at about this time but it was later rebuilt, altering its initially rectangular form so as to be more rounded and, presumably, more authentic-looking. The most military feature of the walls in the 18th century may have been the addition of a magazine for storing powder and shot, just inside the north-east quadrant, documented in 1778.

Some people had an advantage in their requests of the city council. Robert Bull was a successful lawyer who came into an inheritance. In c 1750 he acquired and rebuilt East Pallant house, the gardens of which extended to the south-east quadrant of the city wall, perhaps the largest area of private ground inside the city walls; traces of the clamps for making the bricks for the house have been excavated on the site of the garden. The gardens were interrupted by a public road, possibly a long-established intramural road serving the

defences. Bull was a very rich man (some of his custom-made Oriental china was found in the excavations); he joined the city council, became mayor in 1757 and thereafter was an alderman. On 23 September 1763 Alderman Bull, who leased from the council a property on the wall at the bottom of his garden, possibly a bastion, asked that he be allowed to pull the property down and sell the materials. A month later, on 21 October, he asked the council to block the public road across his garden. Eleven members of the council paid the site a visit and decided unanimously on 24 October that it would be 'no injury or prejudice to the corporation' nor to anyone else to accede to Alderman Bull's requests. (The road, too, was found in excavations, and East Pallant House is now part of the District Council's offices and its gardens are a car park.)

A little lower down the social scale, James Spershott, a local man born in 1710, a joiner by trade and a Baptist pastor by calling, wrote a short memoir of Chichester at the end of the 18th century in which he noted how the prosperity of the city had grown in his lifetime. This betterment was most obviously evident in the rebuilding and refacing of houses, and it is fortunate that brick was the fashionable material in which to carry out this work, rather than stone, otherwise it would have been difficult for the upstanding wall around the city to have survived robbing for its building material. As it was, the wall in much of the south-east

10

quadrant, perhaps not as substantial as the wall and bank elsewhere, was encroached upon and effectively left only as a property boundary. Some of the small squared stones identified as possibly original or early facing stones of the Roman masonry wall are to be seen reused in the walls of the former St Olave's church, North Street, and possibly elsewhere.

Spershott, though he assumed that Chichester's walls were Anglo-Saxon, clearly admired them. He writes in his memoirs with admirable perceptiveness:

And now let us a little reflect on the work of this fortification How great a work to dig the moat, throw up the rampart and prepare the foundation of the wall six foot [1.8m] thick and then built it near 30 foot [9.1m] high with flint stones. And where such a quantity, so many thousands of loads of such large land stones could be collected from, has often been a matter of wonder to me. If from Sellers Park, the Harroways, or Kingly Bottom, the most likely places I can think of, what a number of wains or carts must be employed and w[ha]t expense the whole, adding still almost the same quantity of lime and sand, and the multitude of hands engaged in it.

10 The powder magazine under the steps at East Walls is indicated by the blocked doorway and culvert on the inner face of the wall

11 Chichester in the 18th century

N

north gate
(demolished 1773)

wall ramp used as
raised town walk

north wall walk

wall ramp used as
raised town walk

The Upper West Lane

The Lower West Lane

North Street

Town Hall

THE FRIARY PARK

ditches
filled in

St Peter-the-Less

Crane Lane

west gate
(demolished 1773)

West Street

Custom House Lane

Council House
(1731)

The Friary Park

Friars Lane

St Mary's
Hospital

bell tower

St Olave

St Martin

Little London

Bishop's garden wall
rebuilt in brick
(1771)

cathedral

the Cross

St Andrew

east wall walk

Burying Ground

Bishop's
Palace

cloister

Vicars' Hall

East Street

St Pancras
(rebuilt 1750)

Bishop's
Palace
Gate

Canon Lane

the Deanery
(1725)

All Saints

The North Pallant

River Lavant

Canon Gate

The West Pallant

Baffin's Hall
(Presbyterian chapel, 1721)

site of east gate
and gate gaol
(demolished 1783)
new gaol
(1793)

South Street

The East Pallant

Black
Friars

Baptist chapel
(1671 rebuilt 1728)

The South Pallant
or Plough Lane

Old Theatre
(1761)

south gate
(demolished 1773)

11

0   100m

10

Expansion and conservation

At the beginning of the 19th century, perhaps with renewed prosperity brought during the wars with France from 1793 to 1815, two schemes for urban development were launched in Chichester. The first, called simply New Town, was on land within the south-east quadrant of the walls, formerly given to the Blackfriars, sequestrated in the Reformation and since then a large private house and extensive garden. In 1808 this was sold as 60 building plots laid out along two streets running from north to south. On the east, where adjacent building land ran directly up to the line of the walls, there was no reason to maintain this line as anything other than a property boundary. It is fortunate that there was no attempt to extend the New Town development southwards beyond the walls, although this left an awkwardly oblique southern boundary, as the walls there might then have been obliterated as they were further to the north-east. In fact, in 1816, by amalgamating and exchanging pieces of land, one plot was created that did cross the walls, on which Henry Hobbs built a large, somewhat idiosyncratically planned house, Friary Close. This stands largely on the bank, with

its south-east corner extending over the upstanding wall and incorporating a bastion as a garden feature complete with a grotto passage decorated with inscribed and moulded stones, some of Roman origin perhaps taken from the core of the bastion.

The second development, Somerstown, was notable for being entirely outside the line of the walls, to the north-west. This set a precedent and from that date, 1809, onwards all further large-scale urban development took place outside the long-established historic city. This was vital for the survival of the walls. Infrastructure was more easily built outside the walls, too. Metalled turnpike roads were made that arrived at the gates of Chichester from the north (then the main road from London) and

1   Edward Fuller's map of Chichester, 1820

1

the west. A canal between Dell Quay and a basin south of the city, and from thence to the River Arun to the east, was opened in 1824. This was intended to revitalise the city's economy but it seems mainly to have served to deliver fuel to a gas works, built between the canal basin and the city walls in 1823. Much more important for the city's future was the construction of a railway station further to the south in 1846, on a line running westwards to Portsmouth and Southampton. The local economy, based mainly on farming, was depressed in the years after 1815. Chichester depended on its biweekly livestock market, its functions as an administrative centre for West Sussex and its ecclesiastical status.

In the middle years of the 19th century Chichester may actually have been losing population. The city had for many years been the county town only of the western half of Sussex, the eastern half being administered from Lewes. By comparison with other towns and cities nearby, Chichester was in economic decline. One such place was Portsmouth, to the west, whose excellent harbour had long made it a naval base. More remarkable was Brighton (Sussex), to the east, which had been no more than a small fishing village as recently as the end of the 18th century. By the middle of the 19th century its new railway connections and seaside position confirmed it as a fashionable resort and railway town, and made it the fastest growing town in Sussex. Even small coastal towns with harbours, such as Shoreham and Newhaven (Sussex), to the east, were better placed to attract local and small-scale shipping than was Chichester. The struggle to modernise Chichester was not helped by the conservatism of its civic leaders. Famously, the installation of a mains water supply and mains drainage were matters of controversy. The city did little or nothing to improve the situation until practically forced to do so by the inhabitants' death rate. The biweekly livestock market continued to be held in East Street and North Street until 1872, when a new livestock market was built outside the walls to the east. By the end of the 19th century clean water was piped into

2

3

the city, instead of being taken from wells, and sewers took away both waste water and surface water. New firms grew, the best example being Shippam, whose factory producing potted meat and meat paste was just inside the east gate. As in one or two other places, Shippam linked their properties and processes on both sides of the walls by means of private gates through the walls, although the opening they used had first been made in about 1815.

The conservatism of the cathedral, as well as of the city authorities, may have helped preserve the upstanding city wall, for the south-western and southern stretches formed the boundary of the cathedral close. Legal protection was afforded for the first time to historic monuments deemed to be of national importance, no matter who owned them, when parliament passed the Ancient Monuments Act in 1882, although the city walls of Chichester were not scheduled until 1934. The main task thenceforward was to maintain this ancient monument as it was found. Archaeological investigations also took place, the first in 1885 being undertaken shortly in advance of a visit by members of the British

Archaeological Association and aimed, not unnaturally, at one of the most conspicuous elements of the walls, the bastion on the southern side of the Deanery, called the Residentiary bastion. But this investigation had a definite research objective, to ascertain if the remains of the walls were indeed Roman in origin which happily the investigators were able to confirm. Gordon Hills writing up the results in 1886, mistook the name of Roman Chichester, although, interestingly, this had been correctly identified by the Revd Jeremiah Miles in the 18th century (Chapter 9). The confusion arose because many Roman-period place names, including that of Roman Chichester, are documented in only one or two late Roman itineraries and similar lists, and a misidentification of one place has a knock-on effect on the identification of others in the list. The next year, 1887, the city commemorated Queen Victoria's golden jubilee by creating and planting Jubilee Gardens, taking advantage of a long stretch of the north-east quadrant of the walls as a backdrop. Previously, the gardens of private houses had been allowed to back on to the upstanding wall, around the north-west quadrant for example, and schools and other institutions had been built against the north-east quadrant. Inside the north-

2 The cathedral spire seen from the canal, c 1898
3 Cattle and sheep market in prosperous Chichester, c 1814
4 East Street, c 1870
5 The old Shippam's factory today, just inside the east gate

east quadrant, Priory Park, which had been opened to subscribers in the 19th century, was given by the Duke of Richmond to the city in 1918 as a public park.

Ensuing archaeological interventions, usually in more adventitious circumstances than those of 1885, have also attempted to answer specific questions; unsurprisingly they have also raised more questions. In a sense this collective, cumulative archaeological enterprise constitutes a gradual rediscovery of Chichester's walls, and of the city and its site in general. Successive archaeological interventions are listed in the gazetteer (below). This archaeological rediscovery was beginning, in the last quarter of the 19th century, at the same time as tourism was being made physically easier, first by train, then by buses and bicycles, and latterly by private car; knowledge was sought and disseminated more widely by free public libraries, universal secondary education, cheap paperbacks

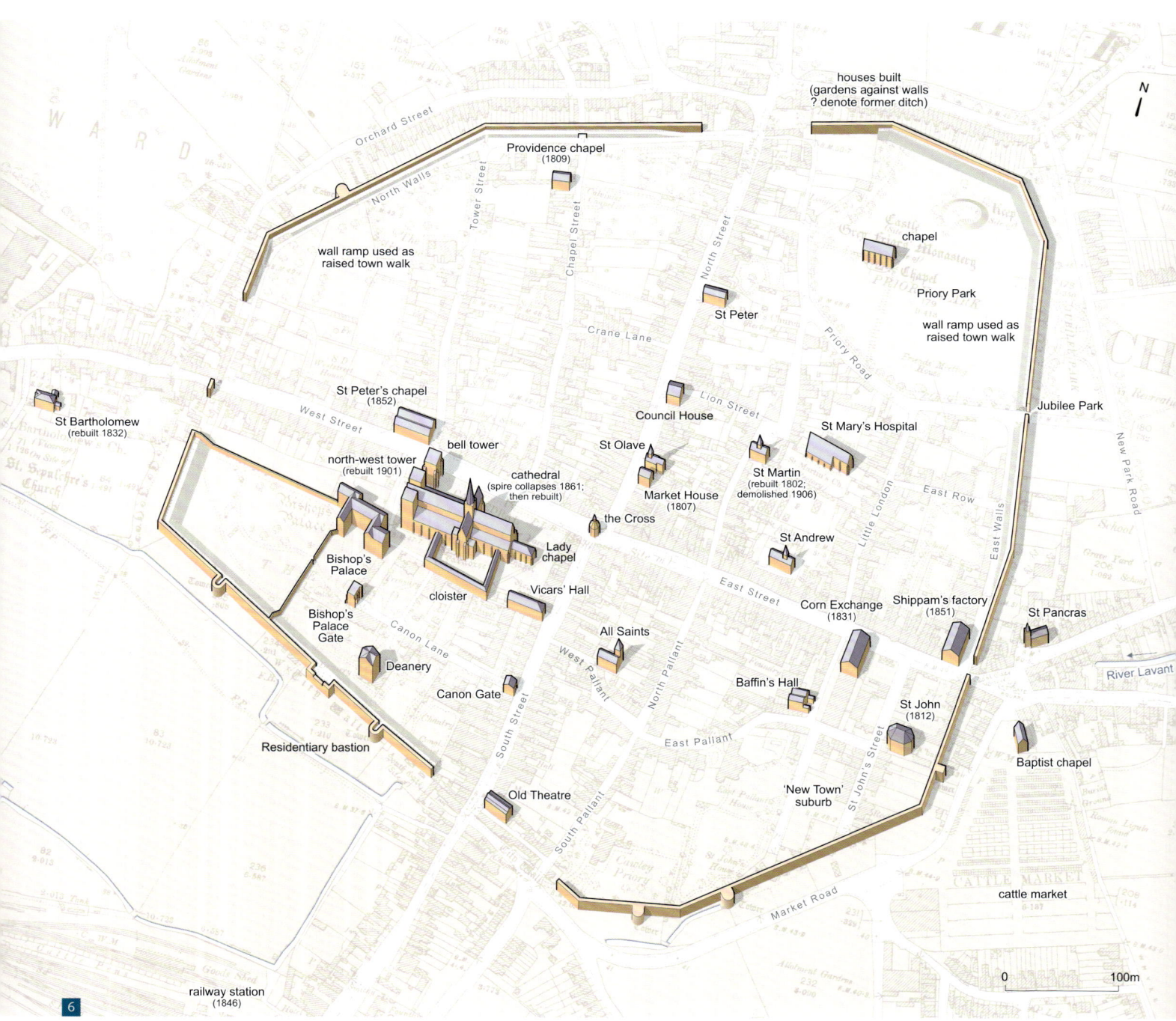

and, since the Second World War, television and wider access to higher education. The cultural context in which the walls exist, and in which they are understood, has become vastly different from what it was at the beginning of, say, the 19th century.

The original wall was much wider and more substantial than it later became (and is now), but it is the case that wherever the inner face of the wall has been exposed the outer footings have either been destroyed or not been accessible, or else the opportunity to determine the original width of the wall has not been taken. Conversely, there have been several archaeological interventions that have exposed the original outer footings but were, perforce, limited to the exterior of the upstanding monument. Excavated sections of the wall indicate a minimum width of 1.8m but the original full width was between 2.4m and 3.0m, where it has recently been measured (Chapter 3).

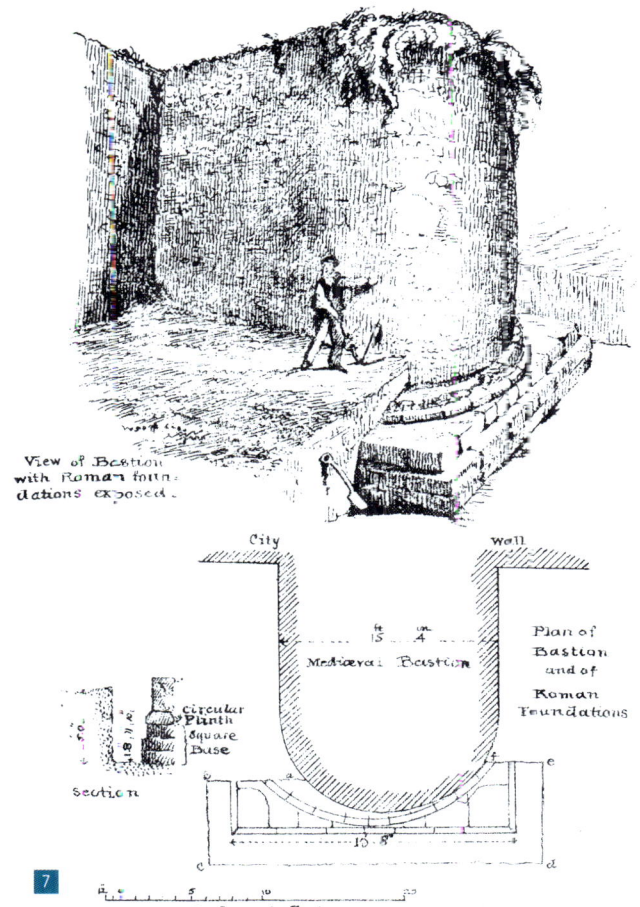

View of Bastion with Roman foundations exposed.

7

6   Chichester in the 19th century

7   Recording of archaeological investigations, published in Gordon Hills' report on the city walls in the *Journal of the British Archaeological Association*, 1886

8   Cricket in Priory Park, perhaps in the 1860s

8

Except for the brick stretch along the west side of the garden of the Bishop's Palace most of the visible upstanding wall is encased in a kind of carapace of flint and hard mortar, surmounted by a thin, plain parapet. Technical documentation may not exist for repairs made before c 1950, but it seems reasonable to suggest that now, early in the 21st century, the masonry wall looks much the same as it has done for at least 200 years, since early in the 19th century, and probably longer. Physically the visible exterior of the wall is, for all practical purposes, quite modern, that is, a modern rebuilding using existing materials if possible. The flint outer face is completely unlike the masonry core behind it, and easily liable to come away. Extensive repairs, usually in response to a sudden fall of the wall face, were carried out in the 1980s and 90s.

The second half of the 20th century has seen two new, quite practical factors affect the walls, both below ground and above ground: the planning system and motor traffic, especially the private car. Greater and more widely distributed affluence in the late 1950s and 1960s was reflected in ownership and use of cars, and heavier traffic. The present planning system was set up during and after the Second World War and the city soon commissioned Thomas Sharp, a pioneer town planner, to write a plan for Chichester. Published in 1949, *Georgian city: a plan for the preservation and improvement of Chichester* emphasised the value of the existing relatively narrow streets and their buildings in the historic city centre, and probably had the effect of preventing wholesale redevelopment taking place there. By the late 1950s and early 1960s specific studies were being undertaken of the effect of more traffic on towns and cities, and how to manage the demand for mobility in such a way that cities could remain liveable. A Royal

Commission studied the problem and issued its report, *Traffic in towns* (also called the Buchanan Report), in 1963, followed in due course by case studies of certain historic towns, of which Chichester was one. In many ways the latter study of Chichester, published in 1968, was a model for its time of assessment of the built heritage in a town, considering what was called streetscape and the group value of urban buildings in all their variety. The study anticipated the designation by local authorities of conservation areas, in addition to the government's listing of individual buildings of special architectural or historic interest, which had come in with the planning system in 1950. The study considered how to divert as much traffic as feasible around the city centre by two ring roads, where to provide car parks, which central streets to give over to pedestrians, how to service shops and businesses in pedestrian streets and how much public transport to provide. This was all put in the context of the existing historic buildings and streets, the attractiveness of which was to be protected and, if possible, enhanced. Ground surfaces and street furniture were also considered.

The historic centre of the city was recognised as being bounded by the city walls, but otherwise the 1968 study paid little attention to them. The walls were taken for granted, perhaps because measures to make them publicly visible and accessible through open space in front of them had already been taken or were in hand; more elements of the walls were scheduled in 1975 and 1983, in addition to those scheduled in 1934. The by-pass to the south of the city centre, constructed in 1939, was widened and then, in accordance with plans drawn up in 1953, supplemented by other new roads. The creation of a roundabout on the site of the west gate in 1964 and construction of an inner ring road (the present Avenue de Chartres), opened in 1965 around the south-west quadrant of the city walls, made the upstanding wall and its prominent bastions more visible to motorists, albeit fleetingly, but arguably diminished the attraction of the views outward from the walls there. Exploiting in this way the open space surviving in front of Chichester's walls was reminiscent of the creation in the 19th century of boulevards in many Continental European cities around the outside or in place of their walls. The 1968 study examined closely what to do with an area in the south-east

9 The west gate, imaginatively reconstructed to celebrate the coronation of King George V in 1911

10 Work on the Palace bastion in 1985 revealed the surviving core of the Roman wall and bastion behind 19th-century facing stones

quarter of the historic centre, East Pallant, which was ripe for redevelopment. Although the walls delimited this particular area to the south-east, the study concentrated on historic buildings there rather than the walls.

'It is not a matter of building a few new roads. It is a matter of dealing with a new social situation. It is not traffic movement, but civilised town life that is at stake': Sir Colin Buchanan was quoted in parliament from his 1957 publication, *Mixed blessing: the motor car in Britain*, when his later report, *Traffic in towns*, was published. As often seems to be the way, ministers, civil servants and parliament were contemplating, and then avoiding or delaying, measures and policies which later came to be seen as absolutely unavoidable, such as urban congestion charges, bus and cycle lanes, park-and-ride schemes, multi-storey car parks near inner-city shopping centres, pedestrian streets and so on. What is striking is how little regard was had in the 1950s and early 1960s for ordinary streets; reconstruction or wholesale re-creation of Britain's provincial cities and towns was thought to be imperative; smaller towns were expected to be able to accommodate road traffic more easily than larger ones; urban renewal, radical modernisation, comprehensive redevelopment and rebuilding, led (?enforced) by

regional development agencies with powers above those of local authorities, would be a cause of national pride. Seen in this light, Chichester was apparently regarded as exceptional at the time, in what was expected to be an ever-expanding economy, and only later has its treatment come to be taken as a model for sustainable development in general in a more conservation-minded age.

To the physical and administrative framework within which the walls exist, determining their future, we must add an intellectual framework of knowledge and understanding. This inevitably is incomplete and in some respects inconsistent and puzzling. From an archaeological point of view, it is just as important to identify periods in which the walls were being severely dilapidated, whether by natural agency or by robbing, as to find out when, by whom and why the walls were built or rebuilt. Logic suggests that these periods of decay should be more or less the converse of the periods of intense construction and repair, but there are some vagaries.

11 Chichester today
12 Busy modern Chichester, with pedestrianised thoroughfares

To sum up, therefore, this archaeological essay proposes the following periods of construction and decay in the history of Chichester's walls.

1   Initial construction of the ditches, bank, masonry wall and gates, probably in the second half of the 3rd century AD.

2   Addition of solid masonry bastion towers to the outer face of the masonry wall, probably in the middle of the 4th century AD.

3   A period of nearly 500 years from the end of the 4th century AD, probably when most damage was done. There may have been human damage at the start, but there is no definite evidence for this, only circumstantial evidence that the south gate may have been blocked. In any case, natural processes left unchecked would probably have been enough to remove the original stone wall faces and crenellated parapets and erode back the core of the upstanding masonry wall and bastion towers to about half their original bulk. Chichester may even owe its English name to the

rubbly appearance of its walls, after this process of dilapidation. If the course of the River Lavant changed at this time to flow around the south-east quadrant of the walls more erosion may have been caused to this quadrant in particular.

4   Adaptation of the walls to form an Anglo-Saxon burh in the AD 870s. A timber palisade may have been added to the masonry wall and bastions, the latter by this time without their original tower-like superstructures. The south-east quadrant was protected by the River Lavant, and this stretch of the walls may have been in worse condition than elsewhere; it was unmanned and may have been left in this condition. The interior of the town was replanned, with a new south gate to the west of the original gate, presumed to have been blocked.

5   From the Norman Conquest of 1066 to the wars with France early in the 13th century, the former burh and Roman defences were of less importance than the motte-and-bailey castle built in the north-east corner of the walled circuit. The town's defences

were probably relatively neglected. The castle's superstructure, which was probably of timber, was dismantled in c 1217–19.

6 After the dismantling of the castle the city would have had more need for its walls, which were rebuilt in bouts of activity prompted by threat of attack from the sea, especially French attacks in the second quarter of the 14th century, at the beginning of the Hundred Years War. The core of the upstanding wall was probably not thickened, but simply refaced and given a new parapet with crenellations. Some of the bastion towers were probably adapted as interval towers, but others may have been pulled down. The original gate openings may have been retained, and new gatehouses built. Special attention was given to rebuilding the south-east quadrant, perhaps no longer so well protected by the Lavant marshes, and possibly weaker anyway than the rest of the circuit.

7 From early in Henry VIII's reign, in 1509, device forts were built on the coast as artillery platforms and warships were developed, in addition to maintaining city walls. Threats of attack by France, Spain and, later, the Netherlands came and went. By about the beginning of the 17th century the ditches were no longer serious obstacles. In the Civil War, in 1642, Royalists took control and reinforced the walls with earth outworks. A Parliamentary

force besieged and bombarded the city; the suburbs were destroyed on the east and west, and the Royalists surrendered. In 1659 the walls were nearly demolished for fear of being taken by the French or another enemy. There may have been few or no crenellations left by this time.

8 From 1660 to 1815 the walls were maintained partly for their diminishing military value and partly for their increasing public amenity value. Tree-shaded walks were made along the top of the upstanding wall, or bank, on the north-west and north-east quadrants comparable to the walks along the edge of the garden of the Bishop's Palace and the Deanery. Several of the bastions were demolished and minor openings made through the wall, particularly after the gates were removed in 1773 and 1783.

9 From 1815 to the present, the walls have had no military value but have been refaced and maintained. Archaeological investigations on modern lines began in 1885, progressively informing the understanding and conservation of the walls as a legally protected monument and a historic symbol of Chichester.

13 **Rebuilding the city walls in the Middle Ages (Fred van Deelen)**
14 **A dated inscription on the brick wall outside the Bishop's Palace garden**

14

1885

Site 1

Residentiary bastion (outer end) foundations exposed (and footings of wall face exposed between 50 feet (15.2m) and 76 feet (23.2m) west of Residentiary bastion, no bastion or ditch found).

Ref: G M Hills, 1886 Chichester: the city walls and their Roman form and foundation, *Journal British Archaeological Association* 42, 119–36: perspective drawing and plan, 118

1932

Site 2

Bank sectioned north of Palace bastion.

Ref: I C Hannah, 1934 The walls of Chichester, *Sussex Archaeological Collections* 75, 107–27: plan and section, 112

Site 3

Palace bastion foundations exposed.

Ref: I C Hannah, 1934 The walls of Chichester, *Sussex Archaeological Collections* 75, 107–27: perspective sketch of west side, looking north, 121; photo of east side, detail of moulded stone, looking north-west, 122

1933

Site 1

Residentiary bastion, outer end, much of east side exposed.

Ref: I C Hannah, 1934 The walls of Chichester, *Sussex Archaeological Collections* 75, 107–27: plan, 124; photo of east side, looking north, 125

Site 4

Bank sectioned, north-west corner of Priory Park.

Ref: I C Hannah, 1934 The walls of Chichester, *Sussex Archaeological Collections* 75, 107–27: section, 116

1947

Sites 5 and 6

Bank sectioned.

Ref: A E Wilson, 1957 Roman Chichester, *Sussex Archaeological Collections* 95, 116–45: esp 119 (site 5 is D and site 6 is E on fig 1, 117)

1949 (or ?1950)

Site 7

Bank sectioned (trench I, Cawley Priory); track east of south gate.

Ref: A Rae, 1951–2 Cawley Priory: wall excavations, *Sussex Archaeological Collections* 90, 179–200: esp 193–4; plan, 180; sections, 181

?1950

Site 8

Tail of bank excavated (trenches II and III, Cawley Priory).

Ref: A H Collins and A E Wilson, 1952 Cawley Priory (sites Aii and Aiii), *Sussex Archaeological Collections* 90, 200–6

?1951

Site 9

Tail of bank excavated (trench IV, Cawley Priory).

Ref: A Rae, 1951–2 Cawley Priory: wall excavations, *Sussex Archaeological Collections* 90, 179–200: plan and section, 198

1952

Sites 10 and 11

Bank sectioned, excavation extended at site 10 to include outer footings of wall and lip of ditch.

Ref: A E Wilson, 1957 Roman Chichester, *Sussex Archaeological Collections* 95, 116–45: esp 119–23 (site 10 is F and site 11 is G on fig 1, 117); sections, 118; photo of inner face of wall at site 11, plate I facing 120

Site 12

East side of Orchard Street bastion excavated, core exposed.

Ref: A E Wilson, 1957 Roman Chichester, *Sussex Archaeological Collections* 95, 116–45: esp 122–3; section, 122

Site 13

Wall face exposed behind Friary Close bastion; some of the wall sectioned and remains of the bastion sectioned and demolished.

Ref: A E Wilson, 1957 Roman Chichester, *Sussex Archaeological Collections* 95, 116–45: esp 123–5; sections, 123; photo plate II facing 121

Site 14

Ditches sectioned in north-east quadrant.

Ref: A E Wilson, 1957 Roman Chichester, *Sussex Archaeological Collections* 95, 116–45: esp 124–5 (site 14 is H on fig 1, 117); section, 124

1956

Site 15

Market Avenue bastion foundations, footings of wall face and lip of ditch exposed.

Ref: A E Wilson, 1957 Roman Chichester, *Sussex Archaeological*

Collections 95, 116–45: esp 125–7 (site 15 is J on fig 1, 117); plan and 'type diagram' section, 126; sections, 128; plate III facing 121

1958

Site 16

Wall partially sectioned in north-east quadrant.

Ref: A E Wilson, 1962 North Walls and Northgate, *Sussex Archaeological Collections* 100, 75–9: esp 75–6; plan and section 76

Site 17

Masonry (? guard room) east of north gate.

Ref: A E Wilson, 1962 North Walls and Northgate, *Sussex Archaeological Collections* 100, 75–9: esp plates I–III between 76 and 77; plan, 78; sections, 79

1959

Sites 7 and 8

Section through bank at Cawley Priory.

Ref: J Holmes, 1962 The defences of Roman Chichester, *Sussex Archaeological Collections* 100, 80–92: section (T3), 87

Site 18

Section through ditches 30 feet (9.1m) to east of Palace bastion.

Ref: J Holmes, 1962 The defences of Roman Chichester, *Sussex Archaeological Collections* 100, 80–92: section (T1) between 80 and 81; plan of bastion, 84

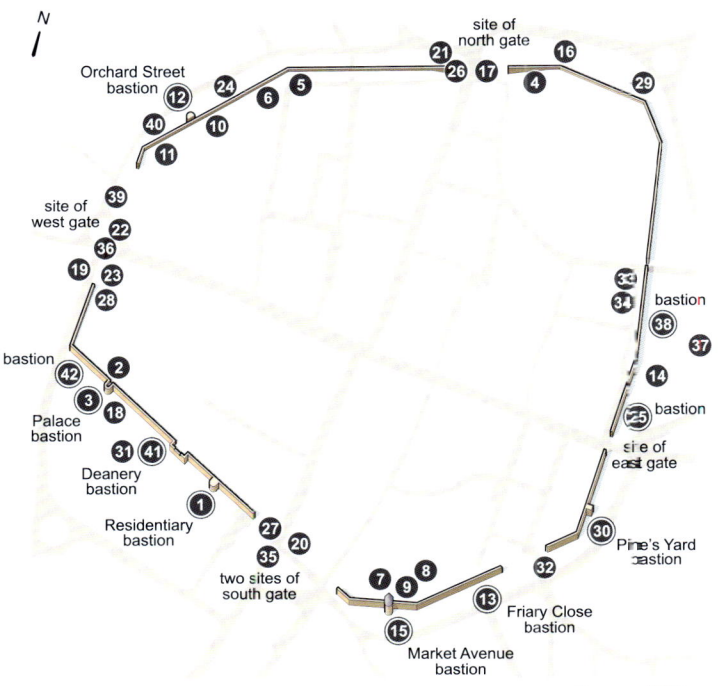

Site 19

Section through ditches in south-west quadrant.

Ref: J Holmes, 1962 The defences of Roman Chichester, *Sussex Archaeological Collections* 100, 80–92: section (T2) between 80 and 81

1960

Site 20

Roman street metalling (excavated by John Holmes) east of Southgate implies position of Roman south gate to east of the medieval south gate and modern South Street.

Ref: J Magilton, 1993 Excavations at Southgate 1960, in A Down and J Magilton, *Chichester excavations 8*, 124–5, Chichester

1962

Site 21

Wall core exposed west of Northgate.

Ref: M Rule, 1971 North Walls and Orchard Street, in A Down and M Rule, *Chichester excavations 1*, 149, Chichester: described only in passing

1964

Site 22

Wall foundations exposed (? to their full width) north of Westgate; pre-defences buildings.

Ref: A Down, 1971 Westgate 1964, in A Down and M Rule, *Chichester excavations 1*, 143–7, Chichester: plan, 144; plan and sections, 145

1966

Site 14

Ditch at Gaumont Cinema.

Ref: M Rule, 1966 Gaumont Cinema site, Eastgate Square, unpublished Chichester District Council report

Site 23

Inner face of wall and bank exposed south of Westgate.

Ref: A Down, 1971 Westgate 1964, in A Down and M Rule, *Chichester excavations 1*, 143–7, Chichester: 147, footnote 4 (ii)

1967–8

Site 24

Wall core exposed behind 104–108 Orchard Street.

Ref: M Rule, 1971 North Walls and Orchard Street, in A Down and M Rule, *Chichester excavations 1*, 149–52, Chichester: section-elevation, 150; plate 2, facing 152

1972

Site 25

Fragment of bastion north of Eastgate; road metalling and northern roadside ditch running north-east from Roman east gate (Stane Street).

Ref: A Down, 1974 The Eastgate bastion, in *Chichester excavations 2*, 59–72, Chichester: plans, 60, 64, 69; sections, 62, 65; plates 7–11 between 62 and 63

1977

Site 26

Masonry at Northgate (? west guard room of the north gate).

Ref: A Down, 1981 Chichester below the streets, in *Chichester excavations 5*, 23–4, Chichester: plan, 24 (no. 107 on fig 2.1, 11)

1979

Site 27

Masonry at Southgate (interpreted initially as east guard room, but later reinterpreted as west guard room in light of site 20).

Ref: A Down, 1981 Chichester below the streets, in *Chichester excavations 5*, 41–4, Chichester: plan (fig 5.16), 42; sections (fig 5.17), 43; reconstruction plan, 44 (no. 132 on fig 2.1, 12; also referred to as 'Southgate 1977' and no. 39)

1981

Site 12

Bastion foundations and wall footings exposed at 92 Orchard Street (excavated by Frances Raymond).

Ref: A Down, 1989 The Roman bastion at Orchard Street, in *Chichester excavations 6*, 26–8, Chichester: plans, 27; section, 28

1985

Site 3

Palace bastion probed, including wall face behind; bastion core partly subsided into pre-defences ?well.

Ref: A Down, 1993 The Palace bastion 1985, in A Down and J Magilton, *Chichester excavations 8*, 114–18, Chichester: plan, section, elevation, 115; plates 116, 117

1987–8

Site 28

Bank sectioned and inner wall face exposed; pre-defences buildings (excavated by John Bowen and Christopher Down).

Ref: J Magilton, 1993 A section through West Walls 1987–8, in A Down and J Magilton, *Chichester excavations 8*, 99–109,

Chichester: plans, 104; section, 100; plates, 101–3

Bank dated to mid–late 3rd century AD instead of late 2nd century AD

Ref: J Kenny, 1993 A summary of the dating evidence, in A Down and J Magilton, *Chichester excavations 8*, 106–8, Chichester; J Magilton, 1993c A section through West Walls 1987–8, in A Down and J Magilton, *Chichester excavations 8*, 99–109, Chichester: esp Discussion, 108–9

1991

Site 29

Wall core and ?medieval outer face exposed at Jubilee Park; two trenches on possible site of bastions but none found.

Ref: R G Browse and J Magilton, 1993 Jubilee Park 1991, in A Down and J Magilton, *Chichester excavations 8*, 109–14, Chichester: plans, 110, 111; section, elevation, 112; plate, 113

Site 30

Possible bastion excavated at Pine's Yard (south-east quadrant); post-medieval in date.

Ref: J Kenny, 1993 Pine's Yard bastion 1991, in A Down and J Magilton, *Chichester excavations 8*, 118–22, Chichester: plans, 119, 121; section, 122; plate, 120

Site 31

Resistivity survey outside the wall to the west of the Old Deanery; interpreted as locating Deanery bastion (but see site 41).

Ref: J Magilton, 1993 A resistivity survey of the Deanery bastion 1991, in A Down and J Magilton, *Chichester excavations 8*, 123–4, Chichester: plans, 123, 124

1996

Site 32

Ditches outside south-east quadrant.

Ref: F Raymond, 2005 River Lavant culvert: excavations in Market Road (St John's Street) car park, Chichester, 1996, *Sussex Archaeological Collections* 142, 45–61

Site 33

Powder magazine at East Walls.

Ref: J Magilton, 1996 A 19th-century powder magazine at East Walls, Chichester, in *The archaeology of Chichester and district: a review of fieldwork and research by Southern Archaeology and others in Chichester District* (ed S Woodward), 29–30, Chichester

1998–9

Site 26

Foundations of the ? north gate.

Ref: J Wildman, 2001 Archaeological monitoring of the mains water renewal scheme, Chichester, West Sussex, unpublished Archaeology South-East report: part 4.9 (no. 31 on fig 4)

Site 34

Pre-defences ? building and street metalling.

Ref: J Wildman, 2001 Archaeological monitoring of the mains water renewal scheme, Chichester, West Sussex, unpublished Archaeology South-East report: part 4.2 (nos 2 and 3 on fig 2)

Site 35

Possible bridge over the River Lavant south of the medieval south gate.

Ref: J Wildman, 2001 Archaeological monitoring of the mains water renewal scheme, Chichester, West Sussex, unpublished Archaeology South-East report: part 4.5 (no. 17 on fig 3)

Site 36

Foundations of the ? west gate and Roman ? street metalling.

Ref: J Wildman, 2001 Archaeological monitoring of the mains water renewal scheme, Chichester, West Sussex, unpublished Archaeology South-East report: part 4.10 (no. 53 on fig 3)

2005

Site 37

Ditches excavated.

Ref: J Taylor, 2005 An archaeological evaluation at East Walls car park, Chichester, West Sussex [site code WEWC05], unpublished Pre-Construct Archaeology Ltd report: section and plan (excludes wall face); J Taylor, 2006 Under the factory floor: excavations at the former Shippam's factory and Shippam's Sports and Social Club,

Chichester, in *Past matters: the heritage of Chichester District*, Heritage annual report 2006 (ed A James), 8–13, Chichester: 6, photo

Site 38

Bastion exposed, ditches excavated, width of wall measured.

Ref: J Taylor, 2005 Shippam's Sports and Social Club East Street, Chichester: archaeological evaluation, unpublished Gifford and Partners Ltd report; Anon, 2006 The bastion discovery, in *Past matters: the heritage of Chichester District*, Heritage annual report 2006 (ed A James), 7, Chichester

Site 39

Wall core exposed; post-medieval robbing of bastion.

Ref: P Hunter and C Pine, 2005 Summary report of the archaeological evaluation at 8 North Walls (Chichester city wall), West Street, Chichester, West Sussex, unpublished Development Archaeology Services report

2008

Site 40

Brick culvert inserted in backfilled ditch.

Ref: M Taylor Sutton, 2008 Results of an archaeological watching brief undertaken at 74–56 Orchard Street, Chichester, West Sussex, unpublished Development Archaeology Services report

2009

Site 41

Bastion located and excavated immediately west of the Old Deanery.

Ref: J Kenny, 2009 A tale of two bastions: investigations on the Chichester city walls, in *Past matters: the heritage of Chichester District* (ed A McQuaid), Heritage annual report 7, 8–9, Chichester

Site 42

Ditches excavated and bastion located west of the Palace bastion.

Ref: J Kenny, 2009 A tale of two bastions: investigations on the Chichester city walls, in *Past matters: the heritage of Chichester District* (ed A McQuaid), Heritage annual report 7, 8–9, Chichester

2010

Site 42

Bastion excavated west of the Palace bastion.

Ref: G Anelay, in prep Community excavations: Bishop's Palace and Old Deanery

15   **Excavation of the bastion west of the Palace bastion in 2010**

Further reading

This book is cast more in the form of an archaeological essay than a monograph and, rather than frequently interrupt the text by citing sources, the most useful sources are mentioned here. An important background document is by J Manley (ed), *The archaeology of Fishbourne and Chichester: a framework for its future* (Lewis, 2008), one of several regional research and conservation frameworks sponsored by English Heritage. Focusing on a study area similar to that of the present book, it succinctly summarises the present state of knowledge of the area from early prehistory to the medieval period, identifies gaps in knowledge, proposes research priorities and includes distribution maps and a valuable bibliography. Four series of publications frequently contain relevant information: *Sussex Archaeological Collections*, the journal of Sussex Archaeological Society, *Chichester excavations* (Chichester, from 1971 onwards) in several volumes, *The archaeology of Chichester and district* (Chichester, from 1985) with an annual gazetteer of discoveries, superseded by, fourthly, *Past matters* (Chichester, from 1998), a more colourful publication which often contains the first notices of discoveries and research results. Previous surveys of Chichester's walls to which the present account is much indebted are those by J Magilton, The defences of Roman Chichester, in *The archaeology of Roman towns: studies in honour of John S Wacher*, edited by P Wilson (156–67, Oxford, 2003), and by A E Wilson, *The archaeology of Chichester city walls* (Chichester Papers 6, Chichester, 1957).

The sources below are described roughly in the order of the chapters of the book to which they are most relevant, but several important sources refer to the walls at more than one period of their history, and these are given only once. The archaeological reports listed in the gazetteer (Chapter 10) often refer to more than one period and are not repeated here.

The Chichester dykes are briefly described by J Magilton (2003, above) and the survey mentioned is reported by R Bradley, A field survey of the Chichester entrenchments, in *Excavations at Fishbourne, 1961–9*, vol 1, edited by B Cunliffe (Society of Antiquaries of London Research Committee Report 26, 17–36, London, 1971). The significance of 'Building 3' at Fishbourne is discussed by J Manley, Measurement and metaphor: the design

and meaning of building 3 at Fishbourne Roman palace, *Sussex Archaeological Collections* 138 (2001), 103–13. The general account of Roman Britain drawn on at many points in this essay is P Salway's *The Oxford illustrated history of Roman Britain* (Oxford, 1993). The possibility that the invasion route was by Chichester, proposed by J G F Hind, The invasion of Britain in AD 43: an alternative strategy for Aulus Plautius, *Britannia* 20 (1989), 1–21, is countered by S Frere and M Fulford, The Roman invasion of AD 43, *Britannia* 32 (2001), 45–55. Extracts about Britain from ancient authors such as Strabo, Tacitus, Dio Cassius, Zosimus and others are to be found in S Ireland (ed), *Roman Britain: a sourcebook* (2nd edition, London, 1996). I Margary's catalogue, *Roman roads in Britain* (3rd edition, London, 1973) is supplemented by J Magilton, Roman roads in the Manhood peninsula, in *The archaeology of Chichester and district: 1995* (31–3, Chichester), D Turner, The course of the Roman road north of Chichester, in *The archaeology of Chichester and district: 1996* (42–7, Chichester) and J Kenny, Roman roads: keeping on the straight and narrow, in *Past matters* 3 (18–21, Chichester, 2005). The possibility of Chichester having a military origin is considered by B Cunliffe, Introduction, in A Down and M Rule, *Chichester excavations 1* (1–7, Chichester, 1971), and underpins A Down's survey of the town, *Roman Chichester* (Chichester, 1988). Excavations at Oaklands Park are

1

reported by A Thorne, Archaeological investigations at the Chichester Festival Theatre, in *Past matters* 6 (13–14, Chichester, 2008). B Cunliffe's reports, *Excavations at Fishbourne, 1961–9* (1971, above) and *Fishbourne Roman palace* (Stroud, 1998) are essential reading. Togidubnus is identified by R S O Tomlin, Reading a 1st-century Roman gold signet ring from Fishbourne, *Sussex Archaeological Collections* 135 (1997), 127–30. For the name of Noviomagus and other places, A L F Rivet and C Smith, *The place-names of Roman Britain* (London, 1979) is the standard work. Evidence to date the origin of the Roman town is discussed by A Down (1988, above), J Magilton (2003, above) and J Wacher, *The towns of Roman Britain* (London, 1974). The suggestion of a theatre in the south-east of the town is by J Kenny, Chichester's first theatre? in *Past matters* 6 (7, Chichester, 2008), and the origin of the castle motte in the north-east is considered by J Magilton, Chichester castle reappears, in *The archaeology of Chichester and district: 1995* (23–6, Chichester). The drawing of the east gate by Grimm is discussed by C G Searle, The appearance of the gates, in A Down, *Chichester excavations 2* (plates 10 and 11 facing 63, and 72–4, Chichester, 1974). The possible quarries for stone are discussed by A Bone and D Bone, Lavant stone: a Roman and medieval building stone in West Sussex, *Sussex Archaeological Collections* 142 (2004), 63–78. Durovernum's defences are described by S S Frere, *Roman Canterbury* (Canterbury, 1962) and S S Frere, S Stow and P Bennett, *Excavations on the Roman defences of Canterbury* (Maidstone, 1982). The dating of Chichester's walls to the late 3rd century is explained by J Kenny, A summary of the dating evidence, in A Down and J Magilton, *Chichester excavations 8* (106–8, Chichester, 1993). Some of the factors in calculating the capacity of beasts of burden are taken from J G Landels, *Engineering in the ancient world* (171–5, London, 1997).

General sources for early Sussex and the English kingdoms are P Hunter Blair, *An introduction to Anglo-Saxon England* (2nd edition, Cambridge, 1977), for towns, D Hill, The origin of the Saxon towns, in *The south Saxons*, edited by P Brandon (174–89, London, 1978), and for the history of Sussex generally, K Leslie and B Short (eds), *An historical atlas of Sussex* (Chichester, 2000). Also useful are P MacDougall, Bosham: a key Anglo-Saxon harbour, *Sussex Archaeological Collections* 147 (2009), 51–60, and J Munby, Saxon Chichester and its predecessors, in *Anglo-Saxon towns in southern England*, edited by J Haslam (315–30, Chichester, 1984). Burhs are located in D Hill's *An atlas of Anglo-Saxon England* (Oxford, 1981). *The life of Bishop Wilfrid by Eddius Stephanus*, edited by B Colgrave (1927) is in paperback (Cambridge, 1985). The standard work,

R G Roberts *The place-names of Sussex* (Cambridge, 1914) gives only the quasi-mythical derivation of the name of Chichester. The course of the River Lavant and its implications for the walls are discussed by J Magilton, Chichester, the Burghal Hidage and the diversion of the River Lavant, in *The archaeology of Chichester and district: 1996* (37–41, Chichester). The Victoria County History (*The Victoria history of the county of Sussex, vol 3: Chichester* (Oxford, 1935)) contains detail for the medieval period as well as the 17th-century Civil War. General points are found in C Creighton and R Higham, *Medieval town walls: an archaeology and social history of urban defence* (Stroud, 2005); information about murage is from H L Turner, *Town defences in England and Wales: an architectural and documentary study, AD 900–1500* (London, 1971); and the events of the 14th century are recounted and analysed by J Sumption, *The Hundred Years War*, especially *Vol 1, Trial by battle* (London, 1990).

Most of the plans relevant to the post-medieval walls are reproduced in D Butler, *The town plans of Chichester, 1595–1898* (Chichester, 1972). A very comprehensive source for all later periods is R Morgan, *Chichester: a documentary history* (Chichester, 1992); the inquest of 1553 is quoted in *Sussex coroners' inquests 1485–1558* (Sussex Record Society 74, Lewes, 1985); visitors' accounts and the petition of 1596 are reproduced in T McCann (ed), *Restricted grandeur: impressions of Chichester 1586–1948* (Chichester, 1974). The minute books of the city council are all in West Sussex Record Office, Chichester. The city of prosperity and gentility is analysed by A H J Green, *The building of Georgian Chichester, 1690–1830* (Chichester, 2007). Comparable development of town walls as public amenities are described in the Royal Commission on Historical Monuments, England, *An inventory of historical monuments in the county of Dorset* (vol 2, part 1, 104–29, London, 1970); *The Victoria history of the county of Chester* (vol 5, part 1, 137–45, Oxford, 2003); P Stamper, *Historic parks and gardens of Shropshire* (36–9, Shrewsbury, 1996); H Conway, *Public parks* (Princes Risborough, 1996); A Taigel and T Williamson, *Know the landscape: parks and gardens* (119–22, London, 1993). Spershott's words are quoted from F W Steer (ed), *The memoirs of James Spershott* (21, 23 Chichester Papers 30, Chichester, 1962). The latest documents cited in the text are C Buchanan, *Traffic in towns: a study of the long-term problems of traffic in urban areas* (London, 1963) and G S Burrows, *Chichester, a study in conservation: report to the Minister of Housing and Local Government* (London, 1968).

The City Walls Project:
its origins and achievements ...

In 2004, as part of a general discussion on the archaeology and history of Chichester's city walls, the District Council's Archaeology Officer and Arts & Heritage Manager agreed that their condition was becoming a cause for concern. As a result of that meeting a Conservation Management Plan was commissioned which made recommendations for the conservation of the walls and improvements to their accessibility. These would entail significant costs, so it was decided to invite interested parties to join a City Walls Partnership whose principal aim would be to secure grant aid for a project aimed at conserving the walls and improving access to them, both intellectual and physical. At the end of 2008 the partnership received confirmation that they had been awarded £685,000 from the Heritage Lottery Fund and a further £199,000 from Chichester District Council to enable the City Walls Project to get underway.

Between 2009 and 2012 structural repairs were undertaken at Westgate Fields, North Walls, Jubilee Park and East Walls. The work included stitching cracks, removing loose flint, raking out defective mortar, repointing with lime mortar and installing structural anchors. Improvements were also made to the paths in Priory Park, Bishop's Palace gardens and alongside the River Lavant.

The project made it possible to research, interpret and promote the archaeology and history of the walls. Achievements included:

• Working with Museum of London Archaeology to publish a detailed account of the walls from the arrival of the Romans to the present day (resulting in this book)

• Installing interpretive plaques, panels and waymarkers to create a 2.4km circular trail around the city

• Creating a new website and adding resources for schools so local children can learn more about the role of the walls in defending the city

• Discovering hidden evidence of life around the walls through geophysical surveys and archaeological excavations undertaken by the local community culminating in a comprehensive report

• Recording for prosperity this moment in time: local people were interviewed as part of an oral history project

• Celebrating the walls with the City Walls Illuminations event in April 2012

• Producing a free leaflet and souvenir guide for residents and visitors to the city.

Visit **www.chichestercitywalls.org** for more information.

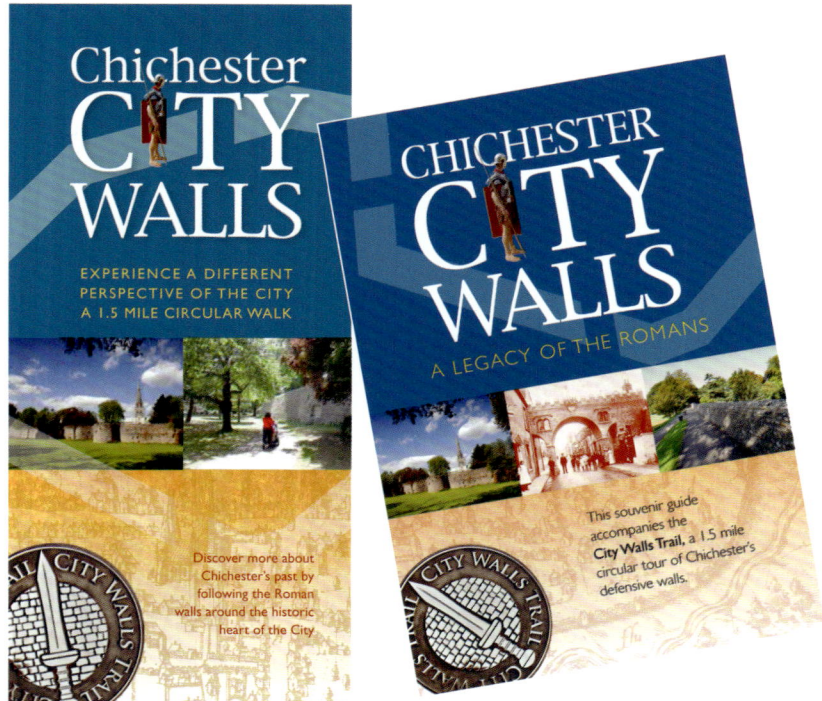

City Walls leaflets and guidebooks are available from The Novium, **www.thenovium.org** 01243 775888

Index